THEODORE ROOSEVELT'S
LETTERS TO HIS CHILDREN

Theodore Roosevelt and his sons (left to right: Theodore, Archie, Quentin, and Kermit) in the White House, 1904

Photo by Arthur Hewitt

THEODORE ROOSEVELT'S
LETTERS TO HIS CHILDREN

EDITED BY
JOSEPH BUCKLIN BISHOP

Guilford, Connecticut

An imprint of The Rowman & Littlefield Publishing Group, Inc.
4501 Forbes Blvd., Ste. 200
Lanham, MD 20706
www.rowman.com

Distributed by NATIONAL BOOK NETWORK

2019 paperback edition published by The Rowman & Littlefield
Publishing Group, Inc.

British Library Cataloguing in Publication Information available

**Library of Congress Cataloging-in-Publication Data
available**

ISBN 978-1-4930-4045-2 (paperback)
ISBN 978-1-4930-4046-9 (e-book)

♾™ The paper used in this publication meets the minimum
requirements of American National Standard for Information
Sciences—Permanence of Paper for Printed Library Materials,
ANSI/NISO Z39.48-1992.

Printed in the United States of America

CONTENTS

	PAGE
INTRODUCTION	3
IN THE SPANISH WAR	13
YOUTHFUL BIBLE COMMENTATORS	17
FINE NAMES FOR GUINEA PIGS	18
A COUGAR AND LYNX HUNT	20
DOGS THAT CLIMB TREES	23
THE PIG NAMED MAUDE	24
ADVICE AND NEWS	25
ARCHIE AND QUENTIN	29
INCIDENTS OF HOME-COMING	30
UNCLE REMUS AND WHITE HOUSE PETS	34
THE DOG "GEM"	35
PRESIDENTIAL NURSE FOR GUINEA PIGS	36
THANKSGIVING IN THE WHITE HOUSE	37
A WHITE HOUSE CHRISTMAS	38
TOM QUARTZ AND JACK	41
A FAR WESTERN TRIP	44
TAME WILD CREATURES	44

CONTENTS

	PAGE
WESTERN CUSTOMS AND SCENERY	44
TREASURES FOR THE CHILDREN	46
MORE TREASURES	47
A HOMESICK PRESIDENT	48
JOSIAH'S PASSIONATE DAY	49
LOVES AND SPORTS OF THE CHILDREN	50
A PRESIDENT AT PLAY	53
TO TED ON A HUNTING TRIP	56
END OF SUMMER AT OYSTER BAY	58
"VALUABLEST" KIND OF RABBITS	59
A PREACHING LETTER	60
PROPER PLACE FOR SPORTS	61
CONCERNING GETTING "SMASHED"	66
THE ART OF UNCLE REMUS	67
A RIDE AND A PILLOW FIGHT	68
STUDY AND PLAY	70
QUENTIN'S FIRST FALL	71
HOMESICK FOR SAGAMORE HILL	73
JOY OVER A FOOTBALL VICTORY	74
VICE-MOTHER OF THE CHILDREN	75
QUENTIN'S SIXTH BIRTHDAY	76
A PRESIDENT'S POOR PROTECTION	77

CONTENTS

	PAGE
TED'S SPRAINED ANKLE	80
THE SUPREME CHRISTMAS JOY	81
A DAY WITH A JUGGLER	82
MERITS OF MILITARY AND CIVIL LIFE	83
ROOT AND TAFT	89
SENATOR HANNA'S DEATH	91
IRRITATING REMARK BY QUENTIN	92
JAPANESE WRESTLING	93
LOVE FOR THE WHITE HOUSE	95
PETER RABBIT'S FUNERAL	96
CHARMS OF VALLEY FORGE	101
WASHINGTON'S COMPANIONS AT VALLEY FORGE	102
ON THE EVE OF NOMINATION FOR PRESIDENT	103
BILL THE LIZARD	105
ON THE EVE OF ELECTION	106
BIG JIM WHITE	109
WINTER LIFE IN THE WHITE HOUSE	110
PLAYMATE OF THE CHILDREN	112
A JAPANESE BOY'S LETTER	113
ON COUNTING DAYS AND WRESTLING	115
SPRING IN WASHINGTON	118
A HUNTING TRIP	119

[vii]

CONTENTS

	PAGE
ABERNETHY THE WOLF HUNTER	121
PRAIRIE GIRLS	124
BEARS, BOBCATS AND SKIP	125
HOME AGAIN WITH SKIP	126
SKIP IN THE WHITE HOUSE	128
OFFICERS OF TOGO'S FLEET	129
A PRESIDENT AS COOK	130
QUENTIN'S QUAINT SAYINGS	134
ADVICE REGARDING NEWSPAPER ANNOYANCES	136
INCIDENTS OF A SOUTHERN TRIP	141
POETS AND PRINCES	144
NOVELS AND GAMES	145
CHRISTMAS PRESENT TO HIS OLD NURSE	148
DICKENS AND THACKERAY	149
A TRIBUTE TO ARCHIE	151
PILLOW FIGHTS WITH THE BOYS	153
SORROWS OF SKIP	155
"AN INTERESTING CIRCUS EXPERIENCE"	156
A BIG AND LONELY WHITE HOUSE	157
A NEW PUPPY AND A NEW HORSE	157
A QUENTIN ANECDOTE	159
A VISIT TO WASHINGTON'S BIRTHPLACE	161

CONTENTS

	PAGE
MORE ABOUT DICKENS	164
NO PLACE LIKE SAGAMORE HILL	165
ATTIC DELIGHTS	166
PRESIDENTIAL RESCUE OF A KITTEN	167
SPORTS OF QUENTIN AND ARCHIE	169
SKIP AND ARCHIE	169
A TURKEY HUNT AT PINE KNOT	170
PETS ON SHIPBOARD	172
NAMES OF THE GUNS	173
REFLECTIONS ON THE WAY	174
EVENTS SINCE COLUMBUS'S DISCOVERY	176
PRIDE IN AMERICA	177
WHAT THE PRESIDENT SAW AT PANAMA	179
ON THE WAY TO PORTO RICO	185
WHAT HE SAW IN PORTO RICO	186
SICKNESS OF ARCHIE	192
AT THE JAMESTOWN EXPOSITION	194
GENERAL KUROKI	196
TEMPORARY ABSENCE OF SKIP	197
DEATH OF SKIP	198
QUENTIN'S SNAKE ADVENTURE	199
TRIALS OF A TRAVELLING PRESIDENT	201

[ix]

CONTENTS

		PAGE
CHANGES OF THREE CENTURIES		202
PECULIARITIES OF MISSISSIPPI STEAMBOATS		206
THE LONE CAT OF THE CAMP		208
SHOOTING THE BEAR		216
QUENTIN'S "EXQUISITE JEST"		217
TOM PINCH		218
"MARTIN CHUZZLEWIT"		219
GOOD READING FOR PACIFISTS		221
QUENTIN AS A BALL-PLAYER		222
FOUR SHEEPISH SMALL BOYS		225
JOHN BURROUGHS AND THE FLYING SQUIRRELS		226
BEAUTY OF WHITE HOUSE GROUNDS		227
QUENTIN AND A BEEHIVE		228
QUENTIN AND TURNER		230
QUENTIN AND THE PIG		231
A PRESIDENTIAL FALL		232
MORE ABOUT QUENTIN		233
TRIBUTE TO KERMIT		236
LONGING FOR HOME		237
THE LAST HUNT		239
QUENTIN GROWN-UP		240

THEODORE ROOSEVELT'S
LETTERS TO HIS CHILDREN

INTRODUCTION

Most of the letters in this volume were written by Theodore Roosevelt to his children during a period of more than a dozen years. A few others are included that he wrote to friends or relatives about the children. He began to write to them in their early childhood, and continued to do so regularly till they reached maturity. Whenever he was separated from them, in the Spanish War, or on a hunting trip, or because they were at school, he sent them these messages of constant thought and love, for they were never for a moment out of his mind and heart. Long before they were able to read he sent them what they called "picture letters," with crude drawings of his own in illustration of the written text, drawings precisely adapted to the childish imagination and intelligence. That the little recipients cherished these delightful missives is shown by the tender care with which they preserved them from destruction. They are in good condition after many years of loving usage. A few of them are reproduced in these pages—written at different periods as each new child appeared in the household.

These early letters are marked by the same quality that distinguishes all his letters to his children. From the youngest to the eldest, he wrote to them always as his equals. As they advanced in life the mental level of intercourse was raised as they grew in intelligence and knowledge, but it was always as equals that he addressed them. He was always their playmate and boon companion, whether they were toddling infants taking their first faltering steps, or growing schoolboys, or youths standing at the threshold of life. Their games were his games, their joys those of his own heart. He was ready to romp with them in the old barn at Sagamore Hill, play "tickley" at bedtime, join in their pillow fights, or play hide-and-seek with them, either at Sagamore Hill or in the White House. He was the same chosen and joyous companion always and everywhere. Occasionally he was disturbed for a moment about possible injury to his Presidential dignity. Describing a romp in the old barn at Sagamore Hill in the summer of 1903, he said in one of his letters that under the insistence of the children he had joined in it because: "I had not the heart to refuse, but really it seems, to put it mildly, rather odd for a stout, elderly President to be bouncing over hayricks in a wild effort to get to goal before an active midget of a competitor, aged nine years. However, it was really great fun."

It was because he at heart regarded it as "great fun" and was in complete accord with the children that they delighted in him as a playmate. In the same spirit, in January, 1905, he took a squad of nine boys, including three of his own, on what they called a "scramble" through Rock Creek Park, in Washington, which meant traversing the most difficult places in it. The boys had permission to make the trip alone, but they insisted upon his company. "I am really touched," he wrote afterward to the parents of two of the

visiting boys, "at the way in which your children
as well as my own treat me as a friend and playmate. It has its comic side. They were all bent
upon having me take them; they obviously felt
that my presence was needed to give zest to the
entertainment. I do not think that one of them
saw anything incongruous in the President's getting as bedaubed with mud as they got, or in my
wiggling and clambering around jutting rocks,
through cracks, and up what were really small
cliff faces, just like the rest of them; and whenever any one of them beat me at any point, he
felt and expressed simple and whole-hearted delight, exactly as if it had been a triumph over a
rival of his own age."

When the time came that he was no longer the
children's chosen playmate, he recognized the fact
with a twinge of sadness. Writing in January,
1905, to his daughter Ethel, who was at Sagamore
Hill at the time, he said of a party of boys that
Quentin had at the White House: "They played
hard, and it made me realize how old I had grown
and how very busy I had been the last few years

to find that they had grown so that I was not needed in the play. Do you recollect how we all of us used to play hide and go seek in the White House, and have obstacle races down the hall when you brought in your friends?"

Deep and abiding love of children, of family and home, that was the dominating passion of his life. With that went love for friends and fellow men, and for all living things, birds, animals, trees, flowers, and nature in all its moods and aspects. But love of children and family and home was above all. The children always had an old-fashioned Christmas in the White House. In several letters in these pages, descriptions of these festivals will be found. In closing one of them the eternal child's heart in the man cries out: "I wonder whether there ever can come in life a thrill of greater exaltation and rapture than that which comes to one between the ages of say six and fourteen, when the library door is thrown open and you walk in to see all the gifts, like a materialized fairy land, arrayed on your special table?"

[7]

His love for the home he had built and in which his beloved children had been born, was not even dimmed by his life in the White House. "After all," he wrote to Ethel in June, 1906, "fond as I am of the White House and much though I have appreciated these years in it, there isn't any place in the world like home—like Sagamore Hill, where things are our own, with their own associations, and where it is real country."

Through all his letters runs his inexhaustible vein of delicious humor. All the quaint sayings of Quentin, that quaintest of small boys; all the antics of the household cats and dogs; all the comic aspects of the guinea-pigs and others of the large menagerie of pets that the children were always collecting; all the tricks and feats of the saddle-horses—these, together with every item of household news that would amuse and cheer and keep alive the love of home in the heart of the absent boys, was set forth in letters which in gayety of spirit and charm of manner have few equals in literature and no superiors. No matter how great the pressure of public duties, or how severe the strain that the trials and burdens of office placed upon the nerves and spirits of the President of a great nation, this devoted father and whole-hearted companion found time to send every week a long letter of this delightful character to each of his absent children.

As the boys advanced toward manhood the letters, still on the basis of equality, contain much wise suggestion and occasional admonition, the latter always administered in a loving spirit accompanied by apology for writing in a "preaching" vein. The playmate of childhood became the sympathetic and keenly interested companion in all athletic contests, in the reading of books and the consideration of authors, and in the discussion of politics and public affairs. Many of these letters, notably those on the relative merits of civil and military careers, and the proper proportions of sport and study, are valuable guides for youth in all ranks of life. The strong, vigorous, exalted character of the writer stands revealed in these as in all the other letters, as well as the cheerful soul of the man which remained throughout his life as pure and gentle as the soul of a child. Only a short time before he died, he said to me, as we were going over the letters and planning this volume, which is arranged as he wished it to be: "I would rather have this book published than anything that has ever been written about me."

THE LETTERS

THE LETTERS

At the outbreak of the war with Spain in the spring of 1898 Theodore Roosevelt, who was then Assistant Secretary of the Navy, in association with Leonard Wood, organized the Regiment of Rough Riders and went into camp with them at Tampa, Florida. Later he went with his regiment to Cuba.

BLESSED BUNNIES,   Camp at Tampa, May 6th, '98.

It has been a real holiday to have darling mother here. Yesterday I brought her out to the camp, and she saw it all—the men drilling, the tents in long company streets, the horses being taken to water, my little horse Texas, the colonel and the majors, and finally the mountain lion and the jolly little dog Cuba, who had several fights while she looked on. The mountain lion is not much more than a kitten as yet, but it is very cross and treacherous.

I was very much interested in Kermit's and Ethel's letters to-day.

[13]

We were all, horses and men, four days and four nights on the cars coming here from San Antonio, and were very tired and very dirty when we arrived. I was up almost all of each night, for it happened always to be at night when we took the horses out of the cars to feed and water them.

Mother stays at a big hotel about a mile from camp. There are nearly thirty thousand troops here now, besides the sailors from the war-ships in the bay. At night the corridors and piazzas are thronged with officers of the army and navy; the older ones fought in the great Civil War, a third of a century ago, and now they are all going to Cuba to war against the Spaniards. Most of them are in blue, but our rough-riders are in brown. Our camp is on a great flat, on sandy soil without a tree, though round about are pines and palmettos. It is very hot, indeed, but there are no mosquitoes. Marshall is very well, and he takes care of my things and of the two horses. A general was out to inspect us when we were drilling to-day.

DARLING ETHEL: Off Santiago, 1898.

We are near shore now and everything is in a bustle, for we may have to disembark to-night, and I do not know when I shall have another chance to write to my three blessed children, whose little notes please me so. This is only a line to tell you all how much father loves you. The Pawnee Indian drew you the picture of the little

dog, which runs everywhere round the ship, and now and then howls a little when the band plays.

[15]

Near Santiago, May 20, 1898.

DARLING ETHEL:

I loved your little letter. Here there are lots of funny little lizards that run about in the dusty roads very fast, and then stand still with their heads up. Beautiful red cardinal birds and tanagers flit about in the woods, and the flowers are lovely. But you never saw such dust. Sometimes I lie on the ground outside and sometimes in the tent. I have a mosquito net because there are so many mosquitoes.

Camp near Santiago, July 15, 1898.

DARLING ETHEL:

When it rains here—and it's very apt to rain here every day—it comes down just as if it was a torrent of water. The other night I hung up my hammock in my tent and in the middle of the night there was a terrific storm, and my tent and hammock came down with a run. The water was running over the ground in a sheet, and the mud was knee-deep; so I was a drenched and muddy object when I got to a neighboring tent, where I was given a blanket, in which I rolled up and went to sleep.

[16]

There is a funny little lizard that comes into my tent and is quite tame now; he jumps about like a little frog and puffs his throat out. There are ground-doves no bigger than big sparrows, and cuckoos almost as large as crows.

YOUTHFUL BIBLE COMMENTATORS
(*To Miss Emily T. Carow*)

Oyster Bay, Dec. 8, 1900.

The other day I listened to a most amusing dialogue at the Bible lesson between Kermit and Ethel. The subject was Joseph, and just before reading it they had been reading Quentin's book containing the adventures of the Gollywogs. Joseph's conduct in repeating his dream to his brothers, whom it was certain to irritate, had struck both of the children unfavorably, as conflicting both with the laws of common-sense and with the advice given them by their parents as to the proper method of dealing with their own brothers and sisters. Kermit said: "Well, I think that was very foolish of Joseph." Ethel chimed in with "So do I, very foolish, and I do not understand how he could have done it." Then, after a pause, Kermit added thoughtfully by way of explanation: "Well, I guess he was simple, like Jane in the Gollywogs": and Ethel nodded gravely in confirmation.

It is very cunning to see Kermit and Archie go to the Cove school together. They also come down and chop with me, Archie being armed with a hatchet blunt enough to be suitable for his six years. He is a most industrious small chopper, and the other day gnawed down, or as the children call it, "beavered" down, a misshapen tulip tree, which was about fifty feet high.

FINE NAMES FOR GUINEA PIGS
(*To E. S. Martin*)

Oyster Bay, Nov. 22, 1900.

Mrs. Roosevelt and I were more touched than I can well say at your sending us your book with its characteristic insertion and above all with the little extract from your boy's note about Ted. In what Form is your boy? As you have laid yourself open, I shall tell you that Ted sings in the choir and is captain of his dormitory football team. He was awfully homesick at first, but now he has won his place in his own little world and he is all right. In his last letter to his mother in response to a question about his clothes he answered that they were in good condition, excepting "that one pair of pants was split up the middle and one jacket had lost a sleeve in a scuffle, and in another pair of pants he had sat down in a jam pie at a cellar spread." We have both missed him greatly in spite of the fact that we have five remaining. Did I ever tell you about my second small boy's names for his Guinea pigs? They included Bishop Doane; Dr. Johnson, my Dutch Reformed pastor; Father G. Grady, the local priest with whom the children had scraped a speaking acquaintance; Fighting Bob Evans, and Admiral Dewey. Some of my Republican supporters in West Virginia have just sent me a small bear which the children of their own accord christened Jonathan Edwards, partly out of compliment to their mother's ancestor, and partly because they thought they detected Calvinistic traits in the bear's character.

A COUGAR AND LYNX HUNT

Keystone Ranch, Colo., Jan. 14th, 1901.

BLESSED TED,

From the railroad we drove fifty miles to the little frontier town of Meeker. There we were met by the hunter Goff, a fine, quiet, hardy fellow, who knows his business thoroughly. Next morning we started on horseback, while our luggage went by wagon to Goff's ranch. We started soon after sunrise, and made our way, hunting as we went, across the high, exceedingly rugged hills, until sunset. We were hunting cougar and lynx or, as they are called out here, "lion" and "cat." The first cat we put up gave the dogs a two hours' chase, and got away among some high cliffs. In the afternoon we put up another, and had a very good hour's run, the dogs baying until the glens rang again to the echoes, as they worked hither and thither through the ravines. We walked our ponies up and down steep, rock-strewn, and tree-clad slopes, where it did not seem possible a horse could climb, and on the level places we got one or two smart gallops. At last the lynx went up

[20]

a tree. Then I saw a really funny sight. Seven hounds had been doing the trailing, while a large brindled bloodhound and two half-breeds between collie and bull stayed behind Goff, running so close to his horse's heels that they continually bumped into them, which he accepted with philosophic composure. Then the dogs proceeded literally to *climb the tree*, which was a many-forked pinon; one of the half-breeds, named Tony, got up certainly sixteen feet, until the lynx, which looked like a huge and exceedingly malevolent pussy-cat, made vicious dabs at him. I shot the lynx low, so as not to hurt his skin.

Yesterday we were in the saddle for ten hours. The dogs ran one lynx down and killed it among the rocks after a vigorous scuffle. It was in a hole and only two of them could get at it.

This morning, soon after starting out, we struck the cold trail of a mountain lion. The hounds puzzled about for nearly two hours, going up and down the great gorges, until we sometimes absolutely lost even the sound of the baying. Then they struck the fresh trail, where the cougar had killed a deer over night. In half an hour a clamorous yelling told us they had overtaken the quarry; for we had been riding up the slopes and along the crests, wherever it was possible for the horses to get footing. As we plunged and scrambled down towards the noise, one of my companions, Phil Stewart, stopped us while he took a kodak of a rabbit which sat unconcernedly right beside our path. Soon we saw the lion in a tree-top, with two of the dogs so high up among the branches that he was striking at them. He was more afraid of us than of the dogs, and as soon as he saw us he took a great flying leap and was off, the pack close behind. In a few hundred yards they had him up another tree. Here I could have shot him (Tony climbed almost up to him, and then fell twenty feet out of the tree), but waited for Stewart to get a photo; and he jumped again. This time, after a couple of hundred yards, the dogs caught him, and a great fight followed. They could have killed him by themselves, but he bit or clawed four of them, and for fear he might kill one I ran in and stabbed him behind the shoulder, thrusting the knife you

[22]

loaned me right into his heart. I have always wished to kill a cougar as I did this one, with dogs and the knife.

DOGS THAT CLIMB TREES

Keystone Ranch, Jan. 18, 1901.

DARLING LITTLE ETHEL:

I have had great fun. Most of the trip neither you nor Mother nor Sister would enjoy; but you would all of you be immensely amused with the dogs. There are eleven all told, but really only eight do very much hunting. These eight are all scarred with the wounds they have received this very week in battling with the cougars and lynxes, and they are always threatening to fight one another; but they are as affectionate toward men (and especially toward me, as I pet them) as our own home dogs. At this moment a large hound and a small half-breed bull-dog, both of whom were quite badly wounded this morning by a cougar, are shoving their noses into my lap to be petted, and humming defiance to one another. They are on excellent terms with the ranch cat and kittens. The three chief fighting

[23]

dogs, who do not follow the trail, are the most affectionate of all, and, moreover, they climb trees! Yesterday we got a big lynx in the top of a pinon tree—a low, spreading kind of pine—about thirty feet tall. Turk, the bloodhound, followed him up, and after much sprawling actually got to the very top, within a couple of feet of him. Then, when the lynx was shot out of the tree, Turk, after a short scramble, took a header down through the branches, landing with a bounce on his back. Tony, one of the half-breed bulldogs, takes such headers on an average at least once for every animal we put up a tree. We have nice little horses which climb the most extraordinary places you can imagine. Get Mother to show you some of Gustave Doré's trees; the trees on these mountains look just like them.

THE PIG NAMED MAUDE

Keystone Ranch, Jan. 29, 1901.

DARLING LITTLE ETHEL:

You would be much amused with the animals round the ranch. The most thoroughly independent and self-possessed of them is a large white pig which we have christened Maude. She goes everywhere at her own will; she picks up scraps from the dogs, who bay dismally at her, but know they have no right to kill her; and then she eats the green alfalfa hay from the two milch cows who live in the big corral with the horses. One of the dogs has just had a litter of puppies; you would love them, with their little wrinkled noses and squeaky voices.

ADVICE AND NEWS

BLESSED TED: Oyster Bay, May 7th, 1901.

It was the greatest fun seeing you, and I really had a satisfactory time with you, and came away feeling that you were doing well. I am entirely satisfied with your standing, both in your studies and in athletics. I want you to do well in your sports, and I want even more to have you do well with your books; but I do not expect you to stand first in either, if so to stand could cause you overwork and hurt your health. I always believe in going hard at everything, whether it is Latin

[25]

or mathematics, boxing or football, but at the same time I want to keep the sense of proportion. It is never worth while to absolutely exhaust one's self or to take big chances unless for an adequate object. I want you to keep in training the faculties which would make you, if the need arose, able to put your last ounce of pluck and strength into a contest. But I do not want you to squander these qualities. To have you play football as well as you do, and make a good name in boxing and wrestling, and be cox of your second crew, and stand second or third in your class in the studies, is all right. I should be rather sorry to see you drop too near the middle of your class, because, as you cannot enter college until you are nineteen, and will therefore be a year later in entering life, I want you to be prepared in the best possible way, so as to make up for the delay. But I know that all you can do you will do to keep substantially the position in the class that you have so far kept, and I have entire trust in you, for you have always deserved it.

The weather has been lovely here. The cherry

trees are in full bloom, the peach trees just open-
ing, while the apples will not be out for ten days.
The May flowers and bloodroot have gone, the
anemonies and bellwort have come and the violets
are coming. All the birds are here, pretty much,
and the warblers troop through the woods.

To my delight, yesterday Kermit, when I tried
him on Diamond, did excellently. He has evidently turned the corner in his riding, and was
just as much at home as possible, although he
was on my saddle with his feet thrust in the
leathers above the stirrup. Poor mother has had
a hard time with Yagenka, for she rubbed her
back, and as she sadly needs exercise and I could
not have a saddle put upon her, I took her out
bareback yesterday. Her gaits are so easy that
it is really more comfortable to ride her without
a saddle than to ride Texas with one, and I gave
her three miles sharp cantering and trotting.

Dewey Jr. is a very cunning white guinea pig.
I wish you could see Kermit taking out Dewey
Sr. and Bob Evans to spend the day on the grass.
Archie is the sweetest little fellow imaginable,

He is always thinking of you. He has now struck up a great friendship with Nicholas, rather to Mame's (the nurse's) regret, as Mame would like to keep him purely for Quentin. The last-named small boisterous person was in fearful disgrace this morning, having flung a block at his mother's head. It was done in sheer playfulness, but of course could not be passed over lightly, and after the enormity of the crime had been brought fully home to him, he fled with howls of anguish to me and lay in an abandon of yellow-headed grief in my arms. Ethel is earning money for the purchase of the Art Magazine by industriously hoeing up the weeds in the walk. Alice is going to ride Yagenka bareback this afternoon, while I try to teach Ethel on Diamond, after Kermit has had his ride.

Yesterday at dinner we were talking of how badly poor Mrs. Blank looked, and Kermit suddenly observed in an aside to Ethel, entirely unconscious that we were listening: "Oh, Effel, I'll tell you what Mrs. Blank looks like: Like Davis' hen dat died—you know, de one dat couldn't hop

up on de perch." Naturally, this is purely a
private anecdote.

Oyster Bay, May 7, 1901.

BLESSED TED:

Recently I have gone in to play with Archie
and Quentin after they have gone to bed, and they
have grown to expect me, jumping up, very soft
and warm in their tommies, expecting me to roll
them over on the bed and tickle and "grabble"
in them.   However, it has proved rather too exciting, and an edict has gone forth that hereafter
I must play bear with them before supper, and
give up the play when they have gone to bed.
To-day was Archie's birthday, and Quentin re-
sented Archie's having presents while he (Quentin) had none.   With the appalling frankness of
three years old, he remarked with great sincerity
that "it made him miserable," and when taken to
task for his lack of altruistic spirit he expressed
an obviously perfunctory repentance and said:
"Well, boys must lend boys things, at any rate!"

INCIDENTS OF HOME-COMING

Oyster Bay, May 31st, 1901.

BLESSED TED:

I enclose some Filipino Revolutionary postage stamps. Maybe some of the boys would like them.

Have you made up your mind whether you would like to try shooting the third week in August or the last week in July, or would you rather wait until you come back when I can find out something more definite from Mr. Post?

We very much wished for you while we were at the (Buffalo) Exposition. By night it was especially beautiful. Alice and I also wished that you could have been with us when we were out riding at Geneseo. Major Wadsworth put me on a splendid big horse called Triton, and sister on a thoroughbred mare. They would jump anything. It was sister's first experience, but she did splendidly and rode at any fence at which I would first put Triton. I did not try anything very high, but still some of the posts and rails were about four feet high, and it was enough to test sister's seat. Of course, all we had to do was to

[30]

stick on as the horses jumped perfectly and enjoyed it quite as much as we did. The first four or five fences that I went over I should be ashamed to say how far I bounced out of the saddle, but after a while I began to get into my seat again. It has been a good many years since I have jumped a fence.

Mother stopped off at Albany while sister went on to Boston, and I came on here alone Tuesday afternoon. St. Gaudens, the sculptor, and Dunne (Mr. Dooley) were on the train and took lunch with us. It was great fun meeting them and I liked them both. Kermit met me in high feather, although I did not reach the house until ten o'clock, and he sat by me and we exchanged anecdotes while I took my supper. Ethel had put an alarm clock under her head so as to be sure and wake up, but although it went off she continued to slumber profoundly, as did Quentin. Archie waked up sufficiently to tell me that he had found another turtle just as small as the already existing treasure of the same kind. This morning Quentin and Black Jack have neither of them been willing to leave me for any length of time. Black Jack simply lies curled up in a chair, but as Quentin is most conversational, he has added an element of harassing difficulty to my effort to answer my accumulated correspondence.

Archie announced that he had seen "the Baltimore orioles catching fish!" This seemed to warrant investigation; but it turned out he meant barn swallows skimming the water.

The President not only sent "picture letters" to his own children, but an especial one to Miss Sarah Schuyler Butler, daughter of Dr. Nicholas Murray Butler, President of Columbia University, who had written to him a little note of congratulation on his first birthday in the White House.

White House, Nov. 3d, 1901.

DEAR LITTLE MISS SARAH,

I liked your birthday note *very* much; and my children say I should draw you two pictures in return.

We have a large blue macaw—Quentin calls

[32]

him a polly-parrot—who lives in the greenhouse, and is very friendly, but makes queer noises. **He** eats bread, potatoes, and coffee grains.

The children have a very cunning pony. **He is** a little pet, like a dog, but he plays tricks **on** them when they ride him.

He bucked Ethel over his head the other **day.**

[33]

Your father will tell you that these are pictures of the UNPOLISHED STONE PERIOD.

Give my love to your mother.

Your father's friend,

THEODORE ROOSEVELT.

UNCLE REMUS AND WHITE HOUSE PETS

(*To Joel Chandler Harris*)

White House, June 9, 1902.

MY DEAR MR. HARRIS:

Your letter was a great relief to Kermit, who always becomes personally interested in his favorite author, and who has been much worried by your sickness. He would be more than delighted with a copy of "Daddy Jake." Alice has it already, but Kermit eagerly wishes it.

Last night Mrs. Roosevelt and I were sitting out on the porch at the back of the White House, and were talking of you and wishing you could be sitting there with us. It is delightful at all times, but I think especially so after dark. The monument stands up distinct but not quite earthly in the night, and at this season the air is sweet with the jasmine and honeysuckle.

[34]

All of the younger children are at present absorbed in various pets, perhaps the foremost of which is a puppy of the most orthodox puppy type. Then there is Jack, the terrier, and Sailor Boy, the Chesapeake Bay dog; and Eli, the most gorgeous macaw, with a bill that I think could bite through boiler plate, who crawls all over Ted, and whom I view with dark suspicion; and Jonathan, the piebald rat, of most friendly and affectionate nature, who also crawls all over everybody; and the flying squirrel, and two kangaroo rats; not to speak of Archie's pony, Algonquin, who is the most absolute pet of them all.

Mrs. Roosevelt and I have, I think, read all your stories to the children, and some of them over and over again.

THE DOG "GEM"

White House, Oct. 13, 1902.

BLESSED KERMIT:

I am delighted at all the accounts I receive of how you are doing at Groton. You seem to be enjoying yourself and are getting on well. I need not tell you to do your best to cultivate ability for concentrating your thought on whatever work you are given to do—you will need it in Latin especially. Who plays opposite you at end? Do you find you can get down well under the ball to tackle the full-back? How are you tackling?

Mother is going to present Gem to Uncle Will. She told him she did not think he was a good dog for the city; and therefore she gives him to Uncle Will to keep in the city. Uncle Will's emotion at such self-denying generosity almost overcame him. Gem is really a very nice small bow-wow, but Mother found that in this case possession was less attractive than pursuit. When she takes him out walking he carries her along as if she was a Roman chariot. She thinks that Uncle Will or Eda can anchor him. Yesterday she and Ethel held him and got burrs out of his hair. It was a lively time for all three.

PRESIDENTIAL NURSE FOR GUINEA PIGS
(To Mrs. Elizabeth Stuart Phelps Ward)

White House, Oct. 20, 1902.

At this moment, my small daughter being out, I am acting as nurse to two wee guinea pigs, which she feels would not be safe save in the room with me—and if I can prevent it I do not intend to have wanton suffering inflicted on any creature.

THANKSGIVING IN THE WHITE HOUSE

White House, Nov. 28, 1902.

DARLING KERMIT:

Yesterday was Thanksgiving, and we all went out riding, looking as we started a good deal like the Cumberbach family. Archie on his beloved pony, and Ethel on Yagenka went off with Mr. Proctor to the hunt. Mother rode Jocko Root, Ted a first-class cavalry horse, I rode Renown, and with us went Senator Lodge, Uncle Douglas, Cousin John Elliott, Mr. Bob Fergie, and General Wood. We had a three hours' scamper which was really great fun.

Yesterday I met Bozie for the first time since he came to Washington, and he almost wiggled himself into a fit, he was so overjoyed at renewing acquaintance. To see Jack and Tom Quartz play together is as amusing as it can be. We have never had a more cunning kitten than Tom

Quartz. I have just had to descend with severity upon Quentin because he put the unfortunate Tom into the bathtub and then turned on the water. He didn't really mean harm.

Last evening, besides our own entire family party, all the Lodges, and their connections, came to dinner. We dined in the new State Dining-room and we drank the health of you and all the rest of both families that were absent. After dinner we cleared away the table and danced. Mother looked just as pretty as a picture and I had a lovely waltz with her. Mrs. Lodge and I danced the Virginia Reel.

A WHITE HOUSE CHRISTMAS

(To Master James A. Garfield, Washington)

White House, Dec. 26, 1902.

JIMMIKINS:

Among all the presents I got I don't think there was one I appreciated more than yours; for I was brought up to admire and respect your grand-father, and I have a very great fondness and esteem for your father. It always seems to me as if you children were being brought up the way that mine are. Yesterday Archie got among his presents a small rifle from me and a pair of riding-boots from his mother. He won't be able to use the rifle until next summer, but he has gone off very happy in the riding boots for a ride on the calico pony Algonquin, the one you rode the other day. Yesterday morning at a quarter of seven all the children were up and dressed and began to hammer at the door of their mother's and my room, in which their six stockings, all bulging out with queer angles and rotundities, were hanging from the fireplace. So their mother and I got up, shut the window, lit the fire, taking down the stockings, of course, put on our wrappers and prepared to admit the children. But first there was a surprise for me, also for their good mother, for Archie had a little Christmas tree of his own which he had rigged up with the help of one of the carpenters in a big closet; and we all had to look at the tree and each of us got a present off of it. There was also one present each for Jack the dog, Tom Quartz the kitten, and Algonquin the pony, whom Archie would no more think of neglecting than I would neglect his brothers and sisters. Then all the children came into our bed and there they opened their stockings. Afterwards we got dressed and took breakfast, and then all went into the library, where each child had a table set for his bigger presents. Quentin had a perfectly delightful electric railroad, which had been rigged up for him by one of his friends, the White House electrician, who has been very good to all the children. Then Ted and I, with General Wood and Mr. Bob Ferguson, who was a lieutenant in my regiment, went for a three hours' ride; and all of us, including all the children, took lunch at the house with the children's aunt, Mrs. Captain Cowles—Archie and Quentin having their lunch at a little table with their cousin Sheffield. Late in the afternoon I played at single stick with General Wood and Mr. Ferguson. I am going to get your father to come on and try it soon. We have to try to hit as light as possible, but sometimes we hit hard, and to-day I have a bump over one eye and a swollen wrist. Then all our family and kinsfolk and Senator and Mrs. Lodge's family and kinsfolk had our Christmas dinner at the White House, and afterwards danced in the East Room, closing up with the Virginia Reel.

TOM QUARTZ AND JACK

White House, Jan. 6, 1903.

DEAR KERMIT:

We felt very melancholy after you and Ted left and the house seemed empty and lonely. But it was the greatest possible comfort to feel that you both really have enjoyed school and are both doing well there.

Tom Quartz is certainly the cunningest kitten I have ever seen. He is always playing pranks on Jack and I get very nervous lest Jack should grow too irritated. The other evening they were both in the library—Jack sleeping before the fire —Tom Quartz scampering about, an exceedingly playful little wild creature—which is about what he is. He would race across the floor, then jump upon the curtain or play with the tassel. Suddenly he spied Jack and galloped up to him. Jack, looking exceedingly sullen and shame-faced, jumped out of the way and got upon the sofa, where Tom Quartz instantly jumped upon him again. Jack suddenly shifted to the other sofa, where Tom Quartz again went after him. Then Jack started for the door, while Tom made a rapid turn under the sofa and around the table, and just as Jack reached the door leaped on his hind-quarters. Jack bounded forward and away and the two went tandem out of the room—Jack not reappearing at all; and after about five minutes Tom Quartz stalked solemnly back.

Another evening the next Speaker of the House, Mr. Cannon, an exceedingly solemn, elderly gentleman with chin whiskers, who certainly does not look to be of playful nature, came to call upon me. He is a great friend of mine, and we sat talking over what our policies for the session should be until about eleven o'clock; and when he went away I accompanied him to the head of the stairs. He had gone about half-way down when Tom Quartz strolled by, his tail erect and very fluffy. He spied Mr. Cannon going down the stairs, jumped to the conclusion that he was a playmate escaping, and raced after him, suddenly grasping him by the leg the way he does Archie and Quentin when they play hide and seek with him; then loosening his hold he tore downstairs ahead of Mr. Cannon, who eyed him with iron calm and not one particle of surprise.

Ethel has reluctantly gone back to boarding-school. It is just after lunch and Dulany is cutting my hair while I dictate this to Mr. Loeb. I left Mother lying on the sofa and reading aloud to Quentin, who as usual has hung himself over the back of the sofa in what I should personally regard as an exceedingly uncomfortable attitude to listen to literature. Archie we shall not see until this evening, when he will suddenly challenge me either to a race or a bear play, and if neither invitation is accepted will then propose that I tell a pig story or else read aloud from the Norse folk tales.

In April, 1903, President Roosevelt made a trip
to the Pacific Coast, visiting Yellowstone Park
and the Grand Canyon of Arizona.

TAME WILD CREATURES

Yellowstone Park, Wyoming,
April 16, 1903.

DARLING ETHEL:

I wish you could be here and see how tame all
the wild creatures are. As I write a dozen of
deer have come down to the parade grounds, right
in front of the house, to get the hay; they are all
looking at the bugler, who has begun to play the
"retreat."

WESTERN CUSTOMS AND SCENERY

Del Monte, Cal., May 10, 1903.

DARLING ETHEL:

I have thought it very good of you to write me
so much. Of course I am feeling rather fagged,
and the next four days, which will include San
Francisco, will be tiresome; but I am very well.
This is a beautiful hotel in which we are spending
Sunday, with gardens and a long seventeen-mile

[44]

drive beside the beach and the rocks and among the pines and cypresses. I went on horseback. My horse was a little beauty, spirited, swift, sure-footed and enduring. As is usually the case here they had a great deal of silver on the bridle and headstall, and much carving on the saddle. We had some splendid gallops. By the way, tell mother that everywhere out here, from the Mississippi to the Pacific, I have seen most of the girls riding astride, and most of the grown-up women. I must say I think it very much better for the horses' backs. I think by the time that you are an old lady the side-saddle will almost have vanished—I am sure I hope so. I have forgotten whether you like the side-saddle or not.

It was very interesting going through New Mexico and seeing the strange old civilization of the desert, and next day the Grand Canyon of Arizona, wonderful and beautiful beyond description. I could have sat and looked at it for days. It is a tremendous chasm, a mile deep and several miles wide, the cliffs carved into battlements, amphitheatres, towers and pinnacles, and the coloring wonderful, red and yellow and gray and green. Then we went through the desert, passed across the Sierras and came into this semi-tropical country of southern California, with palms and orange groves and olive orchards and immense quantities of flowers.

TREASURES FOR THE CHILDREN

Del Monte, Cal., May 10, 1903.

BLESSED KERMIT:

The last weeks' travel I have really enjoyed. Last Sunday and to-day (Sunday) and also on Wednesday at the Grand Canyon I had long rides, and the country has been strange and beautiful. I have collected a variety of treasures, which I shall have to try to divide up equally among you children. One treasure, by the way, is a very small badger, which I named Josiah, and he is now called Josh for short. He is very cunning and I hold him in my arms and pet him. I hope he will grow up friendly—that is if the poor little fellow lives to grow up at all. Dulany is taking excellent care of him, and we feed him on milk and potatoes.

I have enjoyed meeting an old classmate of mine at Harvard. He was heavyweight boxing champion when I was in college.

I was much interested in your seeing the wild deer. That was quite remarkable. To-day, by the way, as I rode along the beach I saw seals, cormorants, gulls and ducks, all astonishingly tame.

MORE TREASURES

Del Monte, Cal., May 10, 1903.

BLESSED ARCHIE:

I think it was very cunning for you and Quentin to write me that letter together. I wish you could have been with me to-day on Algonquin, for we had a perfectly lovely ride. Dr. Rixey and I were on two very handsome horses, with Mexican saddles and bridles; the reins of very slender leather with silver rings. The road led through pine and cypress forests and along the beach. The surf was beating on the rocks in one place and right between two of the rocks where I really did not see how anything could swim a seal appeared and stood up on his tail half out of

[47]

the foaming water and flapped his flippers, and was as much at home as anything could be. Beautiful gulls flew close to us all around, and cormorants swam along the breakers or walked along the beach.

I have a number of treasures to divide among you children when I get back. One of the treasures is Bill the Lizard. He is a little live lizard, called a horned frog, very cunning, who lives in a small box. The little badger, Josh, is very well and eats milk and potatoes. We took him out and gave him a run in the sand to-day. So far he seems as friendly as possible. When he feels hungry he squeals and the colored porters insist that he says "Du-la-ny, Du-la-ny," because Dulany is very good to him and takes care of him.

A HOMESICK PRESIDENT

Del Monte, Cal., May 10, 1903.

DEAREST QUENTY-QUEE:

I loved your letter. I am very homesick for mother and for you children; but I have enjoyed this week's travel. I have been among the orange

[48]

groves, where the trees have oranges growing thick upon them, and there are more flowers than you have ever seen. I have a gold top which I shall give you if mother thinks you can take care of it. Perhaps I shall give you a silver bell instead. Whenever I see a little boy being brought up by his father or mother to look at the procession as we pass by, I think of you and Archie and feel very homesick. Sometimes little boys ride in the procession on their ponies, just like Archie on Algonquin.

JOSIAH'S PASSIONATE DAY

Writing Senator Lodge on June 6, 1903, describing his return to the White House from his western trip, the President said:

"Josiah, the young badger, is hailed with the wildest enthusiasm by the children, and has passed an affectionate but passionate day with us. Fortunately his temper seems proof."

LOVES AND SPORTS OF THE CHILDREN

(*To Miss Emily T. Carow*)

Oyster Bay, Aug. 6, 1903.

To-day is Edith's birthday, and the children have been too cunning in celebrating it. Ethel had hemstitched a little handkerchief herself, and she had taken her gift and the gifts of all the other children into her room and neatly wrapped them up in white paper and tied with ribbons. They were for the most part taken down-stairs and put at her plate at breakfast time. Then at lunch in marched Kermit and Ethel with a cake, burning forty-two candles, and each candle with a piece of paper tied to it purporting to show the animal or inanimate object from which the candle came. All the dogs and horses—Renown, Bleistein, Yagenka, Algonquin, Sailor Boy, Brier, Hector, etc., as well as Tom Quartz, the cat, the extraordinarily named hens—such as Baron Speckle and Fierce, and finally even the boats and that pomegranate which Edith gave Kermit and which has always been known as Santiago, had each his or her or its tag on a special candle.

Edith is very well this summer and looks so young and pretty. She rides with us a great deal and loves Yagenka as much as ever. We also go out rowing together, taking our lunch and a book or two with us. The children fairly worship her, as they ought to, for a more devoted mother never was known. The children themselves are as cunning and good as possible. Ted is nearly as tall as I am and as tough and wiry as you can imagine. He is a really good rider and can hold his own in walking, running, swimming, shooting, wrestling, and boxing. Kermit is as cunning as ever and has developed greatly. He and his inseparable Philip started out for a night's camping in their best the other day. A driving storm came up and they had to put back, really showing both pluck, skill and judgment. They reached home, after having been out twelve hours, at nine in the evening. Archie continues devoted to Algonquin and to Nicholas. Ted's playmates are George and Jack, Aleck Russell, who is in Prince-

ton, and Ensign Hamner of the *Sylph*. They
wrestle, shoot, swim, play tennis, and go off on
long expeditions in the boats. Quenty-quee has
cast off the trammels of the nursery and become
a most active and fearless though very good-
tempered little boy. Really the children do have
an ideal time out here, and it is an ideal place
for them. The three sets of cousins are always
together. I am rather disconcerted by the fact
that they persist in regarding me as a playmate.
This afternoon, for instance, was rainy, and all
of them from George, Ted, Lorraine and Ethel
down to Archibald, Nicholas and Quentin, with
the addition of Aleck Russell and Ensign Hamner, came to get me to play with them in the
old barn. They plead so hard that I finally
gave in, but upon my word, I hardly knew whether
it was quite right for the President to be engaged
in such wild romping as the next two hours saw.
The barn is filled with hay, and of course meets
every requirement for the most active species of
hide-and-seek and the like. Quentin enjoyed the
game as much as any one, and would jump down

from one hay level to another fifteen feet below with complete abandon.

I took Kermit and Archie, with Philip, Oliver and Nicholas out for a night's camping in the two rowboats last week. They enjoyed themselves heartily, as usual, each sleeping rolled up in his blanket, and all getting up at an unearthly hour. Also, as usual, they displayed a touching and firm conviction that my cooking is unequalled. It was of a simple character, consisting of frying beefsteak first and then potatoes in bacon fat, over the camp fire; but they certainly ate in a way that showed their words were not uttered in a spirit of empty compliment.

A PRESIDENT AT PLAY

(To Miss Emily T. Carow)

Oyster Bay, Aug. 16, 1903.

Archie and Nick continue inseparable. I wish you could have seen them the other day, after one of the picnics, walking solemnly up, jointly carrying a basket, and each with a captured turtle in his disengaged hand. Archie is a most warm-hearted, loving, cunning little goose. Quentin, a merry soul, has now become entirely one of the children, and joins heartily in all their plays, including the romps in the old barn. When Ethel had her birthday, the one entertainment for which she stipulated was that I should take part in and supervise a romp in the old barn, to which all the Roosevelt children, Ensign Hamner of the *Sylph*, Bob Ferguson and Aleck Russell were to come. Of course I had not the heart to refuse; but really it seems, to put it mildly, rather odd for a stout, elderly President to be bouncing over hay-ricks in a wild effort to get to goal before an active midget of a competitor, aged nine years. However, it was really great fun.

One of our recent picnics was an innovation, due to Edith. We went in carriages or on horseback to Jane's Hill, some eight miles distant. The view was lovely, and there was a delightful old farmhouse half a mile away, where we left our horses. Speck (German Ambassador, Count Speck von Sternberg) rode with Edith and me, looking more like Hans Christian Andersen's little tin soldier than ever. His papers as Ambassador had finally come, and so he had turned up at Oyster Bay, together with the Acting Secretary of State, to present them. He appeared in what was really a very striking costume, that of a hussar. As soon as the ceremony was over, I told him to put on civilized raiment, which he did, and he spent a couple of days with me. We chopped, and shot, and rode together. He was delighted with Wyoming, and, as always, was extremely nice to the children.

The other day all the children gave amusing amateur theatricals, gotten up by Lorraine and Ted. The acting was upon Laura Roosevelt's tennis court. All the children were most cunning, especially Quentin as Cupid, in the scantiest of pink muslin tights and bodice. Ted and Lorraine, who were respectively George Washington and Cleopatra, really carried off the play. At the end all the cast joined hands in a song and dance, the final verse being devoted especially to me. I love all these children and have great fun with them, and I am touched by the way in which they feel that I am their special friend, champion, and companion.

To-day all, young and old, from the three houses went with us to Service on the great battleship *Kearsarge*—for the fleet is here to be inspected by me to-morrow. It was an impressive sight, one which I think the children will not soon forget. Most of the boys afterward went to lunch with the wretched Secretary Moody on the *Dolphin*. Ted had the younger ones very much on his mind, and when he got back said they had been altogether too much like a March Hare tea-party, as Archie, Nicholas and Oliver were not alive to the dignity of the occasion.

TO TED ON A HUNTING TRIP

Oyster Bay, Aug. 25, 1903.

DEAR TED:

We have thought of you a good deal, of course. I am glad you have my rifle with you—you scamp, does it still have "those associations" which you alleged as the reason why you would value it so much when in the near future I became unable

longer to use it? I do not have very much hope
of your getting a great deal of sport on this trip,
and anything you do get in the way of furred or
feathered game and fishing I shall count as so
much extra thrown in; but I feel the trip will
teach you a lot in the way of handling yourself
in a wild country, as well as of managing horses
and camp outfits—of dealing with frontiersmen,
etc. It will therefore fit you to go on a regular
camping trip next time.

I have sternly refused to allow mother to ride
Wyoming, on the ground that I would not have
her make a martyr of herself in the shape of riding a horse with a single-foot gait, which she so
openly detests. Accordingly, I have had some
long and delightful rides with her, she on Yagenka
and I on Bleistein, while Ethel and Kermit have
begun to ride Wyoming. Kermit was with us
this morning and got along beautifully till we galloped, whereupon Wyoming made up his mind
that it was a race, and Kermit, for a moment or
two, found him a handful.

On Sunday, after we came back from church

and bathed, I rowed mother out to the end of Lloyds Neck, near your favorite camping ground. There we took lunch and spent a couple of hours with our books, reading a little and looking out over the beautiful Sound and at the headlands and white beaches of the coast. We rowed back through a strange, shimmering sunset.

I have played a little tennis since you left. Winty Chandler beat me two sets, but I beat him one. Alex. Russell beat me a long deuce set, 10 to 8. To-day the smaller children held their championship. Nick won a long deuce set from Archie, and to my surprise Oliver and Ethel beat Kermit and Philip in two straight sets. I officiated as umpire and furnished the prizes, which were penknives.

END OF SUMMER AT OYSTER BAY

Oyster Bay, Sept. 23, 1903.

BLESSED KERMIT:

The house seems very empty without you and Ted, although I cannot conscientiously say that it is quiet—Archie and Quentin attend to that.

Archie, barefooted, bareheaded, and with his usual faded blue overalls, much torn and patched, has just returned from a morning with his beloved Nick. Quentin has passed the morning in sports and pastimes with the long-suffering secret service men. Allan has been associating closely with mother and me. Yesterday Ethel went off riding with Lorraine. She rode Wyoming, who is really turning out a very good family horse. This evening I expect Grant La Farge and Owen Wister, who are coming to spend the night. Mother is as busy as possible putting up the house, and Ethel and I insist that she now eyes us both with a purely professional gaze, and secretly wishes she could wrap us up in a neatly pinned sheet with camphor balls inside. Good-bye, blessed fellow!

"VALUABLEST" KIND OF RABBITS

(To his sister, Mrs. W. S. Cowles)

White House, Oct. 2, 1903.

Tell Sheffield that Quentin is now going to the public school. As yet he has preserved an attitude of dignified reserve concerning his feelings on the subject. He has just been presented with two white rabbits, which he brought in while we were at lunch yesterday, explaining that they were "the valuablest kind with pink eyes."

A PREACHING LETTER

White House, Oct. 2, 1903.

DEAR KERMIT:

I was very glad to get your letter. Am glad you are playing football. I should be very sorry to see either you or Ted devoting most of your attention to athletics, and I haven't got any special ambition to see you shine overmuch in athletics at college, at least (if you go there), because I think it tends to take up too much time; but I do like to feel that you are manly and able to hold your own in rough, hardy sports. I would rather have a boy of mine stand high in his studies than high in athletics, but I could a great deal rather have him show true manliness of character than show either intellectual or physical prowess; and I believe you and Ted both bid fair to develop just such character.

There! you will think this a dreadfully preaching letter! I suppose I have a natural tendency to preach just at present because I am overwhelmed with my work. I enjoy being President, and I like to do the work and have my hand on the lever. But it is very worrying and puzzling, and I have to make up my mind to accept every kind of attack and misrepresentation. It is a great comfort to me to read the life and letters of Abraham Lincoln. I am more and more impressed every day, not only with the man's wonderful power and sagacity, but with his literally endless patience, and at the same time his unflinching resolution.

PROPER PLACE FOR SPORTS

DEAR TED: White House, Oct. 4, 1903.

In spite of the "Hurry! Hurry!" on the outside of your envelope, I did not like to act until I had consulted Mother and thought the matter over; and to be frank with you, old fellow, I am by no means sure that I am doing right now. If it were not that I feel you will be so bitterly disappointed, I would strongly advocate your acquiescing in the decision to leave you off the second squad this year. I am proud of your pluck, and I greatly admire football—though it was not a game I was ever able to play myself, my qualities resembling Kermit's rather than yours. But the very things that make it a good game make it a rough game, and there is always the chance of your being laid up. Now, I should not in the least object to your being laid up for a season if you were striving for something worth while, to get on the Groton school team, for instance, or on your class team when you entered Harvard—for of course I don't think you will have the weight to entitle you to try for the 'varsity. But I am by no means sure that it *is* worth your while to run the risk of being laid up for the sake of playing in the second squad when you are a fourth former, instead of when you are a fifth former. I do not know that the risk is balanced by the reward. However, I have told the Rector that as you feel so strongly about it, I think that the chance of your damaging yourself in body is outweighed by the possibility of bitterness of spirit if you could not play. Understand me, I should think mighty little of you if you permitted chagrin to make you bitter on some point where it was evidently right for you to suffer the chagrin. But in this case I am uncertain, and I shall give you the benefit of the doubt. If, however, the coaches at any time come to the conclusion that you ought not to be in the second squad, why you must come off without grumbling.

I am delighted to have you play football. I believe in rough, manly sports. But I do not believe in them if they degenerate into the sole end of any one's existence. I don't want you to sacrifice standing well in your studies to any over-athleticism; and I need not tell you that character counts for a great deal more than either intellect or body in winning success in life. Athletic proficiency is a mighty good servant, and like so many other good servants, a mighty bad master. Did you ever read Pliny's letter to Trajan, in which he speaks of its being advisable to keep the

Greeks absorbed in athletics, because it distracted
their minds from all serious pursuits, including
soldiering, and prevented their ever being dangerous to the Romans? I have not a doubt that
the British officers in the Boer War had their
efficiency partly reduced because they had sacri-
ficed their legitimate duties to an inordinate and
ridiculous love of sports. A man must develop
his physical prowess up to a certain point; but
after he has reached that point there are other
things that count more. In my regiment nine-
tenths of the men were better horsemen than I
was, and probably two-thirds of them better
shots than I was, while on the average they were
certainly hardier and more enduring. Yet after I
had had them a very short while they all knew,
and I knew too, that nobody else could command
them as I could. I am glad you should play
football; I am glad that you should box; I am
glad that you should ride and shoot and walk and
row as well as you do. I should be very sorry if
you did not do these things. But don't ever get
into the frame of mind which regards these things

as constituting the end to which all your energies must be devoted, or even the major portion of your energies.

Yes, I am going to speak at Groton on prize day. I felt that while I was President, and while you and Kermit were at Groton I wanted to come up there and see you, and the Rector wished me to speak, and so I am very glad to accept.

By the way, I am working hard to get Renown accustomed to automobiles. He is such a handful now when he meets them that I seriously mind encountering them when Mother is along. Of course I do not care if I am alone, or with another man, but I am uneasy all the time when I am out with Mother. Yesterday I tried Bleistein over the hurdles at Chevy Chase. The first one was new, high and stiff, and the old rascal never rose six inches, going slap through it. I took him at it again and he went over all right.

I am very busy now, facing the usual endless worry and discouragement, and trying to keep steadily in mind that I must not only be as resolute as Abraham Lincoln in seeking to achieve decent ends, but as patient, as uncomplaining, and as even-tempered in dealing, not only with knaves, but with the well-meaning foolish people, educated and uneducated, who by their unwisdom give the knaves their chance.

.   .   .   .

CONCERNING GETTING "SMASHED"

DEAR TED: White House, Oct. 11, 1903.

I have received letters from the Rector, from Mr. Woods, and from Mr. Billings. They all say that you should play on the third squad, and Mr. Woods says you are now satisfied to do so. This was my first, and as I am convinced, my real judgment in the case. If you get mashed up now in a serious way it may prevent your playing later. As I think I wrote you, I do not in the least object to your getting smashed if it is for an object that is worth while, such as playing on the Groton team or playing on your class team when you get to Harvard. But I think it a little silly to run any imminent risk of a serious smash simply to play on the second squad instead of the third.

[66]

I am judging for you as I would for myself. When I was young and rode across country I was light and tough, and if I did, as actually happened, break an arm or a rib no damage ensued and no scandal was caused. Now I am stiff and heavy, and any accident to me would cause immense talk, and I do not take the chance; simply because it is not worth while. On the other hand, if I should now go to war and have a brigade as I had my regiment before Santiago, I should take any chance that was necessary; because it would be worth while. In other words, I want to make the risk to a certain accident commensurate with the object gained.

THE ART OF UNCLE REMUS

(To Joel Chandler Harris)

MY DEAR HARRIS: White House, Oct. 12, 1901.

It is worth while being President when one's small daughter receives that kind of an autograph gift. When I was younger than she is, my Aunt Annie Bulloch, of Georgia, used to tell me

some of the brer rabbit stories, especially brer
rabbit and the tar baby. But fond though I am
of the brer rabbit stories I think I am even fonder
of your other writings. I doubt if there is a more
genuinely pathetic tale in all our literature than
"Free Joe." Moreover I have felt that all that
you write serves to bring our people closer together. I know, of course, the ordinary talk is
that an artist should be judged purely by his art;
but I am rather a Philistine and like to feel that
the art serves a good purpose. Your art is not
only an art addition to our sum of national
achievement, but it has also always been an addition to the forces that tell for decency, and above
all for the blotting out of sectional antagonism.

A RIDE AND A PILLOW FIGHT

White House, Oct. 19, 1903.

DEAR KERMIT:

I was much pleased at your being made captain of your eleven. I would rather have you
captain of the third eleven than playing on the
second.

Yesterday afternoon Ethel on Wyoming, Mother

on Yagenka and I on Renown had a long ride, the only incident being meeting a large red automobile, which much shook Renown's nerves, although he behaved far better than he has hitherto been doing about automobiles. In fact, he behaved so well that I leaned over and gave him a lump of sugar when he had passed the object of terror— the old boy eagerly turning his head around to get it. It was lovely out in the country, with the trees at their very best of the fall coloring. There are no red maples here, but the Virginia creepers and some of the dogwoods give the red, and the hickories, tulip trees and beeches a brilliant yellow, sometimes almost orange.

When we got home Mother went up-stairs first and was met by Archie and Quentin, each loaded with pillows and whispering not to let me know that they were in ambush; then as I marched up to the top they assailed me with shrieks and chuckles of delight and then the pillow fight raged up and down the hall. After my bath I read them from Uncle Remus. Usually Mother reads them, but now and then, when I think she really must have a holiday from it, I read them myself.

STUDY AND PLAY

White House, Oct. 24, 1903.

DEAR TED:

I am really greatly pleased at your standing so high in your form, and I am sure that this year it is better for you to be playing where you are in football. I suppose next year you will go back to your position of end, as you would hardly be heavy enough for playing back, or to play behind the centre, against teams with big fellows. I repeat that your standing in the class gave me real pleasure. I have sympathized so much with your delight in physical prowess and have been so glad at the success you have had, that sometimes I have been afraid I have failed to emphasize sufficiently the fact that of course one must not subordinate study and work to the cultivation of such prowess. By the way, I am sorry to say that I am falling behind physically. The last two or three years I have had a tendency to rheumatism, or gout, or something of the kind, which makes me very stiff.

Renown is behaving better about automobiles

and the like. I think the difference is largely in the way I handle him. He is a very good-natured and gentle horse, but timid and not over-wise, and when in a panic his great strength makes him well-nigh uncontrollable. Accordingly, he is a bad horse to try to force by anything. If possible, it is much better to give him a little time, and bring him up as gently as may be to the object of terror. When he behaves well I lean forward and give him a lump of sugar, and now the old boy eagerly puts around his head when I stretch out my hand. Bleistein I have ridden very little, because I think one of his forelegs is shaky, and I want to spare him all I can. Mother and I have had the most lovely rides imaginable.

* * * * * * * *

QUENTIN'S FIRST FALL

DEAR KERMIT: White House, Oct. 24, 1903.

Yesterday I felt rather seedy, having a touch of Cuban fever, my only unpleasant reminiscence of the Santiago campaign. Accordingly, I spent the afternoon in the house lying on the sofa, with a

[71]

bright fire burning and Mother in the rocking-
chair, with her knitting, beside me. I felt so glad
that I was not out somewhere in the wilderness,
campaigning or hunting, where I would have to
walk or ride all day in the rain and then lie out
under a bush at night!

When Allan will come from the trainer's I do
not know. Rather to my surprise, Ronald has
won golden opinions and really is a very nice dog.
Pinckney loves him, and he sits up in the express
wagon just as if it was what he had been born to.

Quentin is learning to ride the pony. He had
one tumble, which, he remarked philosophically,
did not hurt him any more than when I whacked
him with a sofa cushion in one of our pillow
fights. I think he will very soon be able to man-
age the pony by himself.

Mother has just taken the three children to
spend the afternoon at Dr. Rixey's farm. I am
hard at work on my message to Congress, and
accordingly shall not try to go out or see any one
either this afternoon or this evening. All of this
work is terribly puzzling at times, but I peg away

at it, and every now and then, when the dust clears away and I look around, I feel that I really have accomplished a little, at any rate.

I think you stood well in your form, taking everything into · account. I feel you deserve credit for being captain of your football eleven, and yet standing as high as you do in your class.

HOMESICK FOR SAGAMORE HILL

DEAR TED: White House, Nov. 4, 1903.

Three cheers for Groton! It was first-class.

On election day I saw the house, and it was all so lovely that I felt fairly homesick to be back in it. The Japanese maples were still in full leaf and were turning the most beautiful shades of scarlet imaginable. The old barn, I am sorry to say, seems to be giving away at one end.

Renown now behaves very well about automobiles, and indeed about everything. He is, however, a little touched in the wind. Bleistein, in spite of being a little shaky in one foreleg, is in splendid spirits and eager for any amount of go.

When you get on here for the Christmas holidays you will have to try them both, for if there is any fox hunting I am by no means sure you will find it better to take Bleistein than Renown.

Sister is very handsome and good, having had a delightful time.

That was a funny trick which the Indians played against Harvard. Harvard did well to play such a successful uphill game in the latter part of the second half as to enable them to win out; but I do not see how she stands a chance of success against Yale this year.

JOY OVER A FOOTBALL VICTORY

White House, Nov. 4, 1903.

DEAR KERMIT:

To-night while I was preparing to dictate a message to Congress concerning the boiling caldron on the Isthmus of Panama, which has now begun to bubble over, up came one of the ushers with a telegram from you and Ted about the football match. Instantly I bolted into the next room to read it aloud to mother and sister, and we all cheered in unison when we came to the Rah! Rah! Rah! part of it. It was a great score. I wish I could have seen the game.

.   .   .   .

VICE-MOTHER OF THE CHILDREN

DEAR KERMIT: White House, Nov. 15, 1903.

Didn't I tell you about Hector, Brier and Sailor Boy (dogs) when I saw them on election day? They were in excellent health, lying around the door of Seaman's house, which they had evidently adopted as their own. Sailor Boy and Brier were exceedingly affectionate; Hector kindly, but uninterested.

Mother has gone off for nine days, and as usual I am acting as vice-mother. Archie and Quentin are really too cunning for anything. Each night I spend about three-quarters of an hour reading to them. I first of all read some book like Algonquin Indian Tales, or the poetry of Scott or Macaulay. Once I read them Jim Bludsoe, which perfectly enthralled them and made Quentin ask me at least a hundred questions, including one as

[75]

to whether the colored boy did not find sitting on the safety valve hot. I have also been reading them each evening from the Bible. It has been the story of Saul, David and Jonathan. They have been so interested that several times I have had to read them more than one chapter. Then each says his prayers and repeats the hymn he is learning, Quentin usually jigging solemnly up and down while he repeats it. Each finally got one hymn perfect, whereupon in accordance with previous instructions from mother I presented each of them with a five-cent piece. Yesterday (Saturday) I took both of them and Ethel, together with the three elder Garfield boys, for a long scramble down Rock Creek. We really had great fun.

QUENTIN'S SIXTH BIRTHDAY

White House, Nov. 19, 1903.

DEAR KERMIT:

I was much pleased at your being chosen captain of the Seventh. I had not expected it. I rather suspect that you will be behind in your studies this month. If so, try to make up next

[76]

month, and keep above the middle of the class if you can. I am interested in what you tell me about the Sir Galahads, and I shall want to talk to you about them when you come on.

Mother is back with Aunt Emily, who looks very well. It is so nice to have her. As for Mother, of course she makes the house feel like a home again, instead of like a temporary dwelling.

Leo is as cunning as ever. Pinckney went to see Allan yesterday and said he found him "as busy as a bee in a tar barrel," and evidently owning all the trainer's house. He is not yet quite fit to come back here.

To-day is Quentin's birthday. He has a cold, so he had his birthday cake, with the six candles, and his birthday ice-cream, in the nursery, with Ethel, Archie, Mother, Aunt Emily, myself, Mame and Georgette as admiring guests and onlookers.

A PRESIDENT'S POOR PROTECTION

DEAR KERMIT: White House, Nov. 28, 1903.

It was very sad at Uncle Gracie's funeral; and yet lovely, too, in a way, for not only all his old

[77]

friends had turned out, but all of the people con-
nected with the institutions for which he had
worked during so many years also came. There
were a good many of the older boys and employees from the Newsboys' Lodging House and the
Orthopædic Dispensary, etc. Uncle Jimmy possessed a singularly loving and affectionate nature,
and I never knew any one who in doing good was
more careful to do it unostentatiously. I had no
idea how much he had done. Mother with her
usual thoughtfulness had kept him steadily in
mind while I have been Governor and President;
and I now find that he appreciated her so much,
her constant remembrances in having him on to
visit us on different occasions. It was a lesson
to me, for I should probably never have thought
of it myself; and of course when one does not do
what one ought to, the excuse that one erred from
thoughtlessness instead of wrong purpose is of
small avail.

The police arrangements at the church were
exasperating to a degree. There were fully five
hundred policemen in the streets round about, just

as if there was danger of an attack by a ferocious mob; and yet though they had throngs of policemen inside, too, an elderly and harmless crank actually got inside with them to present me some foolish memorial about curing the German Emperor from cancer. Inasmuch as what we needed was, not protection against a mob, but a sharp lookout for cranks, the arrangement ought by rights to have been for fifty policemen outside and two or three good detectives inside. I felt like a fool with all the policemen in solemn and purposeless lines around about; and then I felt half exasperated and half amused when I found that they were utterly helpless to prevent a crank from getting inside after all.

P. S.—I enclose two original poems by Nick and Archie. They refer to a bit of unhappy advice I gave them, because of which I fell into richly merited disgrace with Mother. Nick has been spending three days or so with Archie, and I suggested that they should explore the White House in the mirk of midnight. They did, in white sheets, and, like little jacks, barefooted. Send me back the poems.

TED'S SPRAINED ANKLE

White House, Nov. 28, 1903.

DEAR TED:

If I were you I should certainly get the best ankle support possible. You do not want to find next fall that Webb beats you for end because your ankle gives out and his does not. If I were in your place, if it were necessary, I should put the ankle in plaster for the next three weeks, or for as long as the doctor thinks it needful, rather than run any risk of this. At any rate, I would consult him and wear whatever he thinks is the right thing.

.   .   .   .

I wonder if you are old enough yet to care for a good history of the American Revolution. If so, I think I shall give you mine by Sir George Trevelyan; although it is by an Englishman, I really think it on the whole the best account I have read. If I give it to you you must be very careful of it, because he sent it to me himself.

P. S.—The Bond parrot for mother has turned up; it is a most meritorious parrot, very friendly, and quite a remarkable talker.

THE SUPREME CHRISTMAS JOY

(To his sister, Mrs. Douglas Robinson)

White House, Dec. 26, 1903.

. . . .

We had a delightful Christmas yesterday—just such a Christmas thirty or forty years ago we used to have under Father's and Mother's supervision in 20th street and 57th street. At seven all the children came in to open the big, bulgy stockings in our bed; Kermit's terrier, Allan, a most friendly little dog, adding to the children's delight by occupying the middle of the bed. From Alice to Quentin, each child was absorbed in his or her stocking, and Edith certainly managed to get the most wonderful stocking toys. Bob was in looking on, and Aunt Emily, of course. Then, after breakfast, we all formed up and went into the library, where bigger toys were on separate tables for the children. I wonder whether there ever can come in life a thrill of greater exaltation and rapture than that which comes to one between the ages of say six and fourteen, when the library door is thrown open and you walk in to see all the gifts, like a materialized fairy land, arrayed on your special table?

.   .   .   .

A DAY WITH A JUGGLER

DEAR KERMIT: White House, Jan. 18, 1904.

Thursday and Friday there was a great deal of snow on the ground, and the weather was cold, so that Mother and I had two delightful rides up Rock Creek. The horses were clipped and fresh, and we were able to let them go along at a gallop, while the country was wonderfully beautiful.

To-day, after lunch, Mother took Ethel, Archie and Quentin, each with a friend, to see some most wonderful juggling and sleight of hand tricks by Kellar. I went along and was as much interested as any of the children, though I had to come back to my work in the office before it was half through. At one period Ethel gave up her ring for one of

[82]

the tricks. It was mixed up with the rings of five other little girls, and then all six rings were apparently pounded up and put into a pistol and shot into a collection of boxes, where five of them were subsequently found, each tied around a rose. Ethel's, however, had disappeared, and he made believe that it had vanished, but at the end of the next trick a remarkable bottle, out of which many different liquids had been poured, suddenly developed a delightful white guinea pig, squirming and kicking and looking exactly like Admiral Dewey, with around its neck Ethel's ring, tied by a pink ribbon. Then it was wrapped up in a paper, handed to Ethel; and when Ethel opened it, behold, there was no guinea pig, but a bunch of roses with a ring.

MERITS OF MILITARY AND CIVIL LIFE

White House, Jan. 21, 1904.

DEAR TED:

This will be a long business letter. I sent to you the examination papers for West Point and Annapolis. I have thought a great deal over the

[83]

matter, and discussed it at great length with Mother. I feel on the one hand that I ought to give you my best advice, and yet on the other hand I do not wish to seem to constrain you against your wishes. If you have definitely made up your mind that you have an overmastering desire to be in the Navy or the Army, and that such a career is the one in which you will take a really heart-felt interest—far more so than any other—and that your greatest chance for happiness and usefulness will lie in doing this one work to which you feel yourself especially drawn— why, under such circumstances, I have but little to say. But I am not satisfied that this is really your feeling. It seemed to me more as if you did not feel drawn in any other direction, and wondered what you were going to do in life or what kind of work you would turn your hand to, and wondered if you could make a success or not; and that you are therefore inclined to turn to the Navy or Army chiefly because you would then have a definite and settled career in life, and could hope to go on steadily without any great risk of failure. Now, if such is your thought, I shall quote to you what Captain Mahan said of his son when asked why he did not send him to West Point or Annapolis. "I have too much confidence in him to make me feel that it is desirable for him to enter either branch of the service."

I have great confidence in you. I believe you have the ability and, above all, the energy, the perseverance, and the common sense, to win out in civil life. That you will have some hard times and some discouraging times I have no question; but this is merely another way of saying that you will share the common lot. Though you will have to work in different ways from those in which I worked, you will not have to work any harder, nor to face periods of more discouragement. I trust in your ability, and especially your character, and I am confident you will win.

In the Army and the Navy the chance for a man to show great ability and rise above his fellows does not occur on the average more than once in a generation. When I was down at Santiago it was melancholy for me to see how fossil-

ized and lacking in ambition, and generally use-
less, were most of the men of my age and over,
who had served their lives in the Army. The
Navy for the last few years has been better, but
for twenty years after the Civil War there was
less chance in the Navy than in the Army to
practise, and do, work of real consequence. I
have actually known lieutenants in both the
Army and the Navy who were grandfathers—
men who had seen their children married before
they themselves attained the grade of captain.
Of course the chance may come at any time when
the man of West Point or Annapolis who will
have stayed in the Army or Navy finds a great
war on, and therefore has the opportunity to rise
high. Under such circumstances, I think that
the man of such training who has actually left the
Army or the Navy has even more chance of rising
than the man who has remained in it. Moreover,
often a man can do as I did in the Spanish War,
even though not a West Pointer.

This last point raises the question about you
going to West Point or Annapolis and leaving the

Army or Navy after you have served the regulation four years (I think that is the number) after graduation from the academy. Under this plan you would have an excellent education and a grounding in discipline and, in some ways, a testing of your capacity greater than I think you can get in any ordinary college. On the other hand, except for the profession of an engineer, you would have had nothing like special training, and you would be so ordered about, and arranged for, that you would have less independence of character than you could gain from them. You would have had fewer temptations; but you would have had less chance to develop the qualities which overcome temptations and show that a man has individual initiative. Supposing you entered at seventeen, with the intention of following this course. The result would be that at twenty-five you would leave the Army or Navy without having gone through any law school or any special technical school of any kind, and would start your life work three or four years later than your schoolfellows of to-day, who go to work immediately after leaving college. Of course, under such circumstances, you might study law, for instance, during the four years after graduation; but my own feeling is that a man does good work chiefly when he is in something which he intends to make his permanent work, and in which he is deeply interested. Moreover, there will always be the chance that the number of officers in the Army or Navy will be deficient, and that you would have to stay in the service instead of getting out when you wished.

I want you to think over all these matters very seriously. It would be a great misfortune for you to start into the Army or Navy as a career, and find that you had mistaken your desires and had gone in without really weighing the matter.

You ought not to enter unless you feel genuinely drawn to the life as a life-work. If so, go in; but not otherwise.

Mr. Loeb told me to-day that at 17 he had tried for the army, but failed. The competitor who beat him in is now a captain; Mr. Loeb has passed him by, although meanwhile a war has been fought. Mr. Loeb says he wished to enter the army because he did not know what to do, could not foresee whether he would succeed or fail in life, and felt the army would give him "a living and a career." Now if this is at bottom your feeling I should advise you not to go in; I should say yes to some boys, but not to you; I believe in you too much, and have too much confidence in you.

ROOT AND TAFT

DEAR TED: White House, Feb. 6, 1904.

I was glad to hear that you were to be confirmed.

Secretary Root left on Monday and Governor Taft took his place. I have missed, and shall miss, Root dreadfully. He has been the ablest, most generous and most disinterested friend and adviser that any President could hope to have; and immediately after leaving he rendered me a great service by a speech at the Union League Club, in which he said in most effective fashion the very things I should have liked him to say;

and his words, moreover, carried weight as the words of no other man at this time addressing such an audience could have done. Taft is a splendid fellow and will be an aid and comfort in every way. But, as mother says, he is too much like me to be able to give me as good advice as Mr. Root was able to do because of the very differences of character between us.

If after fully thinking the matter over you remain firmly convinced that you want to go into the army, well and good. I shall be rather sorry for your decision, because I have great confidence in you and I believe that in civil life you could probably win in the end a greater prize than will be open to you if you go into the army—though, of course, a man can do well in the army. I know perfectly well that you will have hard times in civil life. Probably most young fellows when they have graduated from college, or from their post-graduate course, if they take any, feel pretty dismal for the first few years. In ordinary cases it at first seems as if their efforts were not leading anywhere, as if the pressure around the foot of the ladder was too great to permit of getting up to the top. But I have faith in your energy, your perseverance, your ability, and your power to force yourself to the front when you have once found out and taken your line. However, you and I and mother will talk the whole matter over when you come back here on Easter.

SENATOR HANNA'S DEATH

White House, Feb. 19, 1904.

DEAR TED:

Poor Hanna's death was a tragedy. At the end he wrote me a note, the last he ever wrote, which showed him at his best, and which I much appreciate. His death was very sad for his family and close friends, for he had many large and generous traits, and had made a great success in life by his energy, perseverance and burly strength.

Buffalo Bill was at lunch the other day, together with John Willis, my old hunter. Buffalo Bill has always been a great friend of mine. I remember when I was running for Vice-President I struck a Kansas town just when the Wild West show was there. He got upon the rear platform of my car and made a brief speech on my behalf, ending with the statement that "a cyclone from the West had come; no wonder the rats hunted their cellars!"

.   .   .   .

As for you, I think the West Point education is, of course, good for any man, but I still think that you have too much in you for me to be glad to see you go into the Army, where in time of peace progress is so much a matter of routine.

IRRITATING REMARK BY QUENTIN

White House, Feb. 27, 1904.

DEAR KERMIT:

Mother went off for three days to New York and Mame and Quentin took instant advantage of her absence to fall sick. Quentin's sickness was surely due to a riot in candy and ice-cream with chocolate sauce. He was a very sad bunny next morning and spent a couple of days in bed. Ethel, as always, was as good as gold both to him and to Archie, and largely relieved me of my

[92]

duties as vice-mother. I got up each morning in time to breakfast with Ethel and Archie before they started for school, and I read a certain amount to Quentin, but this was about all. I think Archie escaped with a minimum of washing for the three days. One day I asked him before Quentin how often he washed his face, whereupon Quentin interpolated, "very seldom, I fear," which naturally produced from Archie violent recriminations of a strongly personal type. Mother came back yesterday, having thoroughly enjoyed Parsifal. All the horses continue sick.

JAPANESE WRESTLING

DEAR KERMIT: White House, March 5, 1904.

.   .   .   .

I am wrestling with two Japanese wrestlers three times a week. I am not the age or the build one would think to be whirled lightly over an opponent's head and batted down on a mattress without damage. But they are so skilful that I have not been hurt at all. My throat is a little sore, because once when one of them had a strangle hold I also got hold of his windpipe and thought I could perhaps choke him off before he could choke me. However, he got ahead.

White House, April 9, 1904.

DEAR TED:

I am very glad I have been doing this Japanese wrestling, but when I am through with it this time I am not at all sure I shall ever try it again while I am so busy with other work as I am now. Often by the time I get to five o'clock in the afternoon I will be feeling like a stewed owl, after an eight hours' grapple with Senators, Congressmen, etc.; then I find the wrestling a trifle too vehement for mere rest. My right ankle and my left wrist and one thumb and both great toes are swollen sufficiently to more or less impair their usefulness, and I am well mottled with bruises elsewhere. Still I have made good progress, and since you left they have taught me three new throws that are perfect corkers.

LOVE FOR THE WHITE HOUSE

White House, May 28, 1904.

DEAR TED:

.　　.　　.　　.　　.　　.　　.　　.

I am having a reasonable amount of work and rather more than a reasonable amount of worry. But, after all, life is lovely here. The country is beautiful, and I do not think that any two people ever got more enjoyment out of the White House than Mother and I. We love the house itself, without and within, for its associations, for its stillness and its simplicity. We love the garden. And we like Washington. We almost always take our breakfast on the south portico now, Mother looking very pretty and dainty in her summer dresses. Then we stroll about the garden for fifteen or twenty minutes, looking at the flowers and the fountain and admiring the trees. Then I work until between four and five, usually having some official people to lunch—now a couple of Senators, now a couple of Ambassadors, now a literary man, now a capitalist or a labor leader,

or a scientist, or a big-game hunter. If Mother
wants to ride, we then spend a couple of hours on
horseback. We had a lovely ride up on the Virginia shore since I came back, and yesterday
went up Rock Creek and swung back home by
the roads where the locust trees were most numer-
ous—for they are now white with blossoms. It
is the last great burst of bloom which we shall see
this year except the laurels. But there are plenty
of flowers in bloom or just coming out, the honeysuckle most conspicuously. The south portico is
fragrant with that now. The jasmine will be out
later. If we don't ride I walk or play tennis.
But I am afraid Ted has gotten out of his father's
class in tennis!

PETER RABBIT'S FUNERAL

DEAR KERMIT: White House, May 28, 1904.

It was great fun seeing you and Ted, and I
enjoyed it to the full.

Ethel, Archie and Quentin have gone to Mount
Vernon to-day with the Garfield boys. Yester-

day poor Peter Rabbit died and his funeral was held with proper state. Archie, in his overalls, dragged the wagon with the little black coffin in which poor Peter Rabbit lay. Mother walked behind as chief mourner, she and Archie solemnly exchanging tributes to the worth and good qualities of the departed. Then he was buried, with a fuchsia over the little grave.

You remember Kenneth Grahame's account of how Harold went to the circus and sang the great spheral song of the circus? Well, yesterday Mother leaned out of her window and heard Archie, swinging under a magnolia tree, singing away to himself, "I'm going to Sagamore, to Sagamore, to Sagamore. I'm going to Sagamore, oh, to Sagamore!" It was his spheral song of joy and thanksgiving.

The children's delight at going to Sagamore next week has completely swallowed up all regret at leaving Mother and me. Quentin is very cunning. He and Archie love to play the hose into the sandbox and then, with their thigh rubber boots on, to get in and make fortifications. Now and then they play it over each other. Ethel is playing tennis quite a good deal.

I think Yagenka is going to come out all right, and Bleistein, too. I have no hope for Wyoming or Renown. Fortunately, Rusty is serving us well.

White House, June 12th, 1904.

BLESSED QUENTY-QUEE:

The little birds in the nest in the vines on the garden fence are nearly grown up. Their mother still feeds them.

You see the mother bird with a worm in her beak, and the little birds with their beaks wide open!

I was out walking the other day and passed the

Zoo; there I fed with grass some of the two-year-old elk; the bucks had their horns "in the velvet." I fed them through the bars.

White House, June 12th, 1904.

BLESSED ARCHIE-KINS:

Give my love to Mademoiselle; I hope you and Quenty are *very* good with her—and don't play in the library!

I loved your letter, and think you were very good to write.

All kinds of live things are sent me from time

[99]

to time. The other day an eagle came; this morning an owl.

(I have drawn him holding a rat in one claw.) We sent both to the Zoo.

The other day while walking with Mr. Pinchot and Mr. Garfield we climbed into the Blagden deer park and almost walked over such a pretty wee fawn, all spotted; it ran off like a little race horse.

It made great jumps and held its white tail straight in the air.

[100]

Dear Quentyquee: White House, June 21, 1904.

The other day when out riding what should I see in the road ahead of me but a real B'rer Terrapin and B'rer Rabbit. They were sitting sol-

emnly beside one another and looked just as if they had come out of a book; but as my horse walked along B'rer Rabbit went lippity lippity lippity off into the bushes and B'rer Terrapin drew in his head and legs till I passed.

CHARMS OF VALLEY FORGE

Dearest Ethel: White House, June 21, 1904.

I think you are a little trump and I love your letter, and the way you take care of the children and keep down the expenses and cook bread and are just your own blessed busy cunning self.

[101]

You would have enjoyed being at Valley Forge with us on Sunday. It is a beautiful place, and, of course, full of historic associations. The garden here is lovely. A pair of warbling vireos have built in a linden and sing all the time. The lindens, by the way, are in bloom, and Massachusetts Avenue is fragrant with them. The magnolias are all in bloom, too, and the jasmine on the porch.

WASHINGTON'S COMPANIONS AT VALLEY FORGE

DEAR TED: White House, June 21, 1904.

Mother and I had a most lovely ride the other day, way up beyond Sligo Creek to what is called North-west Branch, at Burnt Mills, where is a beautiful gorge, deep and narrow, with great boulders and even cliffs. Excepting Great Falls it is the most beautiful place around here. Mother scrambled among the cliffs in her riding habit, very pretty and most interesting. The roads were good and some of the scenery really beautiful. We were gone four hours, half an hour being occupied with the scrambling in the gorge.

[102]

Saturday we went to the wedding of Teddy Douglas and Helen. It was a beautiful wedding in every way and I am very fond of both of them. Sunday we spent at Attorney-General Knox's at Valley Forge, and most unexpectedly I had to deliver a little address at the church in the afternoon, as they are trying to build a memorial to Washington. Think of the fact that in Washington's army that winter among the junior officers were Alexander Hamilton, Monroe and Marshall—a future President of the United States, the future Chief Justice who was to do such wonderful work for our Government, and the man of most brilliant mind—Hamilton—whom we have ever developed in this country.

ON THE EVE OF NOMINATION FOR PRESIDENT

DEAR KERMIT: White House, June 21, 1904.

We spent to-day at the Knoxes'. It is a beautiful farm—just such a one as you could run. Phil Knox, as capable and efficient as he is diminutive, amused Mother and me greatly by the silent way in which he did in first-rate way his full share of all the work.

To-morrow the National Convention meets, and barring a cataclysm I shall be nominated. There is a great deal of sullen grumbling, but it has taken more the form of resentment against what they think is my dictation as to details than against me personally. They don't dare to oppose me for the nomination and I suppose it is hardly likely the attempt will be made to stampede the Convention for any one. How the election will turn out no man can tell. Of course I hope to be elected, but I realize to the full how very lucky I have been, not only to be President but to have been able to accomplish so much while President, and whatever may be the outcome, I am not only content but very sincerely thankful for all the good fortune I have had. From Panama down I have been able to accomplish certain things which will be of lasting importance in our history. Incidentally, I don't think that any family has ever enjoyed the White House more than we have. I was thinking about

June 22d
1904

Darling Ethel,

Here goes for the picture letter!

Ethel administers necessary discipline to Archie and Quentin.

Ethel gives sick Vagenk
a bottle of medicine

Father plays tennis
with Mr. Cooley. ——
[Father's shape & spectacles are reproduce
[with photographic fidelity; also no

Leo chases a squirrel
which fortunately he can't catch

A nice policeman feeding
a squirrel with bread;
I fed two with bread
this afternoon.

Mr. coolys smile

There! My invention has given out; Mother & Aunt Emily have been on a picnic down the river with several cronies we have been sitting on the portico in the moonlight; Sister is _very_ good.

Your loving
father

it just this morning when Mother and I took breakfast on the portico and afterwards walked about the lovely grounds and looked at the stately historic old house. It is a wonderful privilege to have been here and to have been given the chance to do this work, and I should regard myself as having a small and mean mind if in the event of defeat I felt soured at not having had more instead of being thankful for having had so much.

BILL THE LIZARD

BLESSED ARCHIKINS: White House, June 21, 1904.

The other day when Mother and I were walking down the steps of the big south porch we saw a movement among the honeysuckles and there was Bill the lizard—your lizard that you brought home from Mount Vernon. We have seen him several times since and he is evidently entirely at home here. The White House seems big and empty without any of you children puttering around it, and I think the ushers miss you very much. I play tennis in the late afternoons unless I go to ride with Mother.

White House, Oct. 15, 1904.

DARLING KERMIT:

The weather has been beautiful the last week—
mild, and yet with the true feeling of Fall in the
air. When Mother and I have ridden up Rock
Creek through the country round about, it has
been a perpetual delight just to look at the foliage.
I have never seen leaves turn more beautifully.
The Virginia creepers and some of the maple and
gum trees are scarlet and crimson. The oaks are
deep red brown. The beeches, birches and hickories are brilliant saffron. Just at this moment I
am dictating while on my way with Mother to
the wedding of Senator Knox's daughter, and the
country is a blaze of color as we pass through it,
so that it is a joy to the eye to look upon it. I
do not think I have ever before seen the colorings
of the woods so beautiful so far south as this.
Ted is hard at work with Matt. Hale, who is a
very nice fellow and has become quite one of the
household, like good Mademoiselle. I am really
fond of her. She is so bright and amusing and

now seems perfectly happy, and is not only devoted to Archie and Quentin but is very wise in the way she takes care of them. Quentin, under parental duress, rides Algonquin every day. Archie has just bought himself a football suit, but I have not noticed that he has played football as yet. He is spending Saturday and Sunday out at Dr. Rixey's. Ted plays tennis with Matt. Hale and me and Mr. Cooley. We tried Dan Moore. You could beat him. Yesterday I took an afternoon off and we all went for a scramble and climb down the other side of the Potomac from Chain Bridge home. It was great fun. To-morrow (Sunday) we shall have lunch early and spend the afternoon in a drive of the entire family, including Ethel, but not including Archie and Quentin, out to Burnt Mills and back. When I say we all scrambled along the Potomac, I of course only meant Matt. Hale and Ted and I. Three or four active male friends took the walk with us.

In politics things at the moment seem to look quite right, but every form of lie is being circulated by the Democrats, and they intend undoubtedly to spring all kinds of sensational un-truths at the very end of the campaign. I have not any idea whether we will win or not. Before election I shall send you my guess as to the way the different States will vote, and then you can keep it and see how near to the truth I come. But of course you will remember that it is a mere guess, and that I may be utterly mistaken all along the line. In any event, even if I am beaten you must remember that we have had three years of great enjoyment out of the Presidency and that we are mighty lucky to have had them.

I generally have people in to lunch, but at din-ner, thank fortune, we are usually alone. Though I have callers in the evening, I generally have an hour in which to sit with Mother and the others up in the library, talking and reading and watch-ing the bright wood fire. Ted and Ethel, as well as Archie and Quentin, are generally in Mother's room for twenty minutes or a half hour just before she dresses, according to immemorial custom.

Last evening Mother and I and Ted and Ethel

and Matt. Hale went to the theatre to see "The Yankee Consul," which was quite funny.

BIG JIM WHITE

White House, Dec. 3, 1904.

BLESSED KERMIT:

The other day while Major Loeffler was marshalling the usual stream of visitors from England, Germany, the Pacific slope, etc., of warm admirers from remote country places, of bridal couples, etc., etc., a huge man about six feet four, of middle age, but with every one of his great sinews and muscles as fit as ever, came in and asked to see me on the ground that he was a former friend. As the line passed he was introduced to me as Mr. White. I greeted him in the usual rather perfunctory manner, and the huge, rough-looking fellow shyly remarked, "Mr. Roosevelt, maybe you don't recollect me. I worked on the roundup with you twenty years ago next spring. My outfit joined yours at the mouth of the Box Alder." I gazed at him, and at once said, "Why it is big Jim." He was a great cow-

[109]

puncher and is still riding the range in north-western Nebraska. When I knew him he was a tremendous fighting man, but always liked me. Twice I had to interfere to prevent him from half murdering cowboys from my own ranch. I had him at lunch, with a mixed company of home and foreign notabilities.

Don't worry about the lessons, old boy. I know you are studying hard. Don't get cast down. Sometimes in life, both at school and afterwards, fortune will go against any one, but if he just keeps pegging away and doesn't lose his courage things always take a turn for the better in the end.

WINTER LIFE IN THE WHITE HOUSE

White House, Dec. 17, 1904.

BLESSED KERMIT:

For a week the weather has been cold—down to zero at night and rarely above freezing in the shade at noon. In consequence the snow has lain well, and as there has been a waxing moon I have had the most delightful evening and night rides imaginable. I have been so busy that I have been unable to get away until after dark, but I went in the fur jacket Uncle Will presented to me as the fruit of his prize money in the Spanish War; and the moonlight on the glittering snow made the rides lovelier than they would have been in the daytime. Sometimes Mother and Ted went with me, and the gallops were delightful. To-day it has snowed heavily again, but the snow has been so soft that I did not like to go out, and besides I have been worked up to the limit. There has been skating and sleigh-riding all the week.

The new black "Jack" dog is becoming very much at home and very fond of the family.

With Archie and Quentin I have finished "The Last of the Mohicans," and have now begun "The Deerslayer." They are as cunning as ever, and this reading to them in the evening gives me a chance to see them that I would not otherwise have, although sometimes it is rather hard to get time.

Mother looks very young and pretty. This

afternoon she was most busy, taking the little boys to the theatre and then going to hear Ethel sing. Ted, very swell in his first tail coat, is going out to take supper at Secretary Morton's, whose pretty daughter is coming out to-night.

In a very few days now we shall see you again.

PLAYMATE OF THE CHILDREN

(To Mr. and Mrs. Emlen Roosevelt)

White House, Jan. 4, 1905.

I am really touched at the way in which your children as well as my own treat me as a friend and playmate. It has its comic side. Thus, the last day the boys were here they were all bent upon having me take them for a scramble down Rock Creek. Of course, there was absolutely no reason why they could not go alone, but they obviously felt that my presence was needed to give zest to the entertainment. Accordingly, off I went, with the two Russell boys, George, Jack, and Philip, and Ted, Kermit, and Archie, with one of Archie's friends—a sturdy little boy who, as Archie informed me, had played opposite to him in the position of centre rush last fall. I do not think that one of them saw anything incongruous in the President's getting as bedaubed with mud as they got, or in my wiggling and clambering around jutting rocks, through cracks, and up what were really small cliff faces, just like the rest of them; and whenever any one of them beat me at any point, he felt and expressed simple and whole-hearted delight, exactly as if it had been a triumph over a rival of his own age.

A JAPANESE BOY'S LETTER

(*To Dr. William Sturgis Bigelow*)

DEAR STURGIS: White House, Jan. 14, 1905.

Last year, when I had Professor Yamashita teach me the "Jiudo"—as they seem now to call Jiu Jitsu—the naval attaché here, Commander Takashita, used to come around here and bring a young lad, Kitgaki, who is now entering Annapolis. I used to wrestle with them both. They were very fond of Archie and were very good to him. This Christmas Kitgaki sent from Annapolis a little present to Archie, who wrote to thank him, and Kitgaki sent him a letter back that we like so much that I thought you might enjoy it,

[113]

as it shows so nice a trait in the Japanese character. It runs as follows:

"My dearest boy:

"I received your nice letter. I thank you ever so much. I am very very glad that you have receive my small present.

"I like you very very much. When I have been in Jiudo room with your father and you, your father was talking to us about the picture of the caverly officer. In that time, I saw some expression on your face. Another remembering of you is your bravery when you sleped down from a tall chair. The two rememberings can't leave from my head.

"I returned here last Thursday and have plenty lesson, so my work is hard, hard, hard, more than Jiudo.

"I hope your good health.

"I am,

"Sincerely yours,

"A. KITGAKI."

Isn't it a nice letter?

THINKING TOO MUCH OF HOME

White House, Feb. 24, 1905.

DARLING KERMIT:

I puzzled a good deal over your marks. I am inclined to think that one explanation is that you have thought so much of home as to prevent your really putting your whole strength into your studies. It is most natural that you should count the days before coming home, and write as you do that it will only be 33 days, only 26 days, only 19 days, etc., but at the same time it seems to me that perhaps this means that you do not really put all your heart and all your head effort into your work; and that if you are able to, it would be far better to think just as little as possible about coming home and resolutely set yourself to putting your best thought into your work. It is an illustration of the old adage about putting your hand to the plow and then looking back. In after life, of course, it is always possible that at some time you may have to go away for a year or two from home to do some piece of work. If during that whole time you only thought day

[115]

after day of how soon you would get home I think you would find it difficult to do your best work; and maybe this feeling may be partly responsible for the trouble with the lessons at school.

Wednesday, Washington's Birthday, I went to Philadelphia and made a speech at the University of Pennsylvania, took lunch with the Philadelphia City Troop and came home the same afternoon with less fatigue than most of my trips cost me; for I was able to dodge the awful evening banquet and the night on the train which taken together drive me nearly melancholy mad. Since Sunday we have not been able to ride. I still box with Grant, who has now become the champion middle-weight wrestler of the United States. Yesterday afternoon we had Professor Yamashita up here to wrestle with Grant. It was very interesting, but of course jiu jitsu and our wrestling are so far apart that it is difficult to make any comparison between them. Wrestling is simply a sport with rules almost as conventional as those of tennis, while jiu jitsu is really meant for practice in killing or disabling our adversary. In consequence,

Grant did not know what to do except to put Yamashita on his back, and Yamashita was perfectly content to be on his back. Inside of a minute Yamashita had choked Grant, and inside of two minutes more he got an elbow hold on him that would have enabled him to break his arm; so that there is no question but that he could have put Grant out. So far this made it evident that the jiu jitsu man could handle the ordinary wrestler. But Grant, in the actual wrestling and throwing was about as good as the Japanese, and he was so much stronger that he evidently hurt and wore out the Japanese. With a little practice in the art I am sure that one of our big wrestlers or boxers, simply because of his greatly superior strength, would be able to kill any of those Japanese, who though very good men for their inches and pounds are altogether too small to hold their own against big, powerful, quick men who are as well trained.

SPRING IN WASHINGTON

White House, March 20, 1905.

DEAR KERMIT:

Poor John Hay has been pretty sick. He is going away to try to pick up his health by a sea voyage and rest. I earnestly hope he succeeds, not only because of my great personal fondness for him, but because from the standpoint of the nation it would be very difficult to replace him. Every Sunday on my way home from church I have been accustomed to stop in and see him. The conversation with him was always delightful, and during these Sunday morning talks we often decided important questions of public policy.

I paid a scuttling visit to New York on Friday to give away Eleanor at her marriage, and to make two speeches—one to the Friendly Sons of St. Patrick and one to the Sons of the American Revolution.

Mother and I have been riding a good deal, and the country is now lovely. Moreover, Ted and Matt and I have begun playing tennis.

The birds have come back. Not only song-

[118]

sparrows and robins, but a winter wren, purple finches and tufted titmice are singing in the garden; and the other morning early Mother and I were waked up by the loud singing of a cardinal bird in the magnolia tree just outside our windows.

Yesterday afternoon Archie and Quentin each had a little boy to see him. They climbed trees, sailed boats in the fountain, and dug in the sandbox like woodcocks.

Poor Mr. Frank Travers died last night. I was very sorry. He has been a good friend to me.

A HUNTING TRIP

Colorado Springs, Colorado,
April 14, 1905.

BLESSED KERMIT:

I hope you had as successful a trip in Florida as I have had in Texas and Oklahoma. The first six days were of the usual Presidential tour type, but much more pleasant than ordinarily, because I did not have to do quite as much speaking, and there was a certain irresponsibility about it all, due I suppose in part to the fact that I am no longer a candidate and am free from the everlasting suspicion and ill-natured judgment which being a candidate entails. However, both in Kentucky, and especially in Texas, I was received with a warmth and heartiness that surprised me, while the Rough Riders' reunion at San Antonio was delightful in every way.

Then came the five days wolf hunting in Oklahoma, and this was unalloyed pleasure, except for my uneasiness about Auntie Bye and poor little Sheffield. General Young, Dr. Lambert and Roly Fortescue were each in his own way just the nicest companions imaginable, my Texas hosts were too kind and friendly and open-hearted for anything. I want to have the whole party up at Washington next winter. The party got seventeen wolves, three coons, and any number of rattlesnakes. I was in at the death of eleven wolves. The other six wolves were killed by members of the party who were off with bunches of dogs in some place where I was not. I never took part in a run which ended in the death of a wolf without getting through the run in time to see the death. It was tremendous galloping over cut banks, prairie dog towns, flats, creek bottoms, everything. One run was nine miles long and I was the only man in at the finish except the professional wolf hunter Abernethy, who is a really wonderful fellow, catching the wolves alive by thrusting his gloved hands down between their jaws so that they cannot bite. He caught one wolf alive, tied up this wolf, and then held it on the saddle, followed his dogs in a seven-mile run and helped kill another wolf. He has a pretty wife and five cunning children of whom he is very proud, and introduced them to me, and I liked him much. We were in the saddle eight or nine hours every day, and I am rather glad to have thirty-six hours' rest on the cars before starting on my Colorado bear hunt.

ABERNETHY THE WOLF HUNTER

Glenwood Springs, Colorado,
April 20, 1905.

DEAR TED:

I do wish you could have been along on this trip. It has been great fun. In Oklahoma our party got all told seventeen coyotes with the greyhounds. I was in at the death of eleven, the only ones started by the dogs with which I happened to be. In one run the three Easterners covered themselves with glory, as Dr. Lambert, Roly Fortescue and I were the only ones who got through excepting Abernethy, the wolf hunter. It happened because it was a nine-mile run and all the cowboys rode their horses to a standstill in the first three or four miles, after which I came bounding along, like Kermit in the paper chase, and got to the end in time to see the really remarkable feat of Abernethy jumping on to the wolf, thrusting his gloved hand into its mouth, and mastering it then and there. He never used a knife or a rope in taking these wolves, seizing them by sheer quickness and address and thrusting his hand into the wolf's mouth in such a way that it lost all power to bite. You would have loved Tom Burnett, the son of the big cattle man. He is a splendid fellow, about thirty years old, and just the ideal of what a young cattle man should be.

Up here we have opened well. We have two cracker jacks as guides—John Goff, my old guide on the mountain lion hunt, and Jake Borah, who has somewhat the Seth Bullock type of face. We have about thirty dogs, including one absurd little terrier about half Jack's size, named Skip. Skip trots all day long with the hounds, excepting when he can persuade Mr. Stewart, or Dr. Lambert, or me to take him up for a ride, for which he is always begging. He is most affectionate and intelligent, but when there is a bear or lynx at bay he joins in the fight with all the fury of a bull dog, though I do not think he is much more effective than one of your Japanese mice would be. I should like to bring him home for Archie or Quentin. He would go everywhere with them and would ride Betsy or Algonquin.

On the third day out I got a fine big black bear, an old male who would not tree, but made what they call in Mississippi a walking bay with the dogs, fighting them off all the time. The chase lasted nearly two hours and was ended by a hard scramble up a canyon side; and I made a pretty good shot at him as he was walking off with the pack around him. He killed one dog and crippled three that I think will recover, besides scratching others. My 30–40 Springfield worked to perfection on the bear.

I suppose you are now in the thick of your studies and will have but little time to rest after the examinations. I shall be back about the 18th, and then we can take up our tennis again. Give my regards to Matt.

I am particularly pleased that Maurice turned out so well. He has always been so pleasant to me that I had hoped he would turn out all right in the end.

PRAIRIE GIRLS

Divide Creek, Colo., April 26, 1905.

DARLING ETHEL:

Of course you remember the story of the little prairie girl. I always associate it with you. Well, again and again on this trip we would pass through prairie villages—bleak and lonely—with all the people in from miles about to see me. Among them were often dozens of young girls, often pretty, and as far as I could see much more happy

[124]

than the heroine of the story. One of them shook
hands with me, and then, after much whispering,
said: "We want to shake hands with the guard!"
The "guard" proved to be Roly, who was very
swell in his uniform, and whom they evidently
thought much more attractive than the President, both in age and looks.

There are plenty of ranchmen round here; they
drive over to camp to see me, usually bringing a
cake, or some milk and eggs, and are very nice
and friendly. About twenty of the men came
out with me, "to see the President shoot a bear";
and fortunately I did so in the course of an exhausting twelve hours' ride. I am very homesick for you all.

BEARS, BOBCATS AND SKIP

Glenwood Springs, Colorado,
May 2, 1905.

BLESSED KERMIT:

I was delighted to get your letter. I am sorry
you are having such a hard time in mathematics,
but hope a couple of weeks will set you all right.
We have had a very successful hunt. All told we

have obtained ten bear and three bobcats. Dr.
Lambert has been a perfect trump. He is in the
pink of condition, while for the last week I have
been a little knocked out by the Cuban fever.
Up to that time I was simply in splendid shape.
There is a very cunning little dog named Skip, be-
longing to John Goff's pack, who has completely
adopted me. I think I shall take him home to
Archie. He likes to ride on Dr. Lambert's horse,
or mine, and though he is not as big as Jack,
takes eager part in the fight with every bear and
bobcat.

I am sure you will enjoy your trip to Deadwood
with Seth Bullock, and as soon as you return
from Groton I shall write to him about it. I
have now become very homesick for Mother, and
shall be glad when the 12th of May comes and I
am back in the White House.

HOME AGAIN WITH SKIP

White House, May 14, 1905.

DEAR KERMIT:

Here I am back again, and mighty glad to be
back. It was perfectly delightful to see Mother

and the children, but it made me very homesick for you. Of course I was up to my ears in work as soon as I reached the White House, but in two or three days we shall be through it and can settle down into our old routine.

Yesterday afternoon we played tennis, Herbert Knox Smith and I beating Matt and Murray. To-day I shall take cunning mother out for a ride.

Skip accompanied me to Washington. He is not as yet entirely at home in the White House and rather clings to my companionship. I think he will soon be fond of Archie, who loves him dearly. Mother is kind to Skip, but she does not think he is an aristocrat as Jack is. He is a very cunning little dog all the same.

Mother walked with me to church this morning and both the past evenings we have been able to go out into the garden and sit on the stone benches near the fountain. The country is too lovely for anything, everything being a deep, rich, fresh green.

I had a great time in Chicago with the labor

union men. They made what I regarded as a
rather insolent demand upon me, and I gave them
some perfectly straight talk about their duty and
about the preservation of law and order. The
trouble seems to be increasing there, and I may
have to send Federal troops into the city—though
I shall not do so unless it is necessary.

SKIP IN THE WHITE HOUSE

DEAR KERMIT: White House, May 14, 1905.

That was a good mark in Latin, and I am
pleased with your steady improvement in it.

Skip is housebroken, but he is like a real little
Indian. He can stand any amount of hard work
if there is a bear or bobcat ahead, but now that
he is in the White House he thinks he would much
rather do nothing but sit about all day with his
friends, and threatens to turn into a lapdog. But
when we get him to Oyster Bay I think we can
make him go out riding with us, and then I think
he will be with Archie a great deal. He and Jack
are rather jealous of one another. He is very

[128]

cunning and friendly. I am immensely pleased with Mother's Virginia cottage and its name. I am going down there for Sunday with her some time soon.

P. S.—Your marks have just come! By George, you have worked hard and I am delighted. Three cheers!

OFFICERS OF TOGO'S FLEET

DEAR KERMIT: White House, June 6, 1905.

Next Friday I am going down with Mother to spend a couple of days at Pine Knot, which Mother loves just as Ethel loves Fidelity. She and I have had some lovely rides together, and if I do not go riding with her I play tennis with Ted and some of his and my friends. Yesterday Ted and one of his friends played seven sets of tennis against Mr. Cooley and me and beat us four to three. In the evening Commander Takashita brought in half a dozen Japanese naval officers who had been with Togo's fleet off Port Arthur and had taken part in the fleet actions, the attacks with the torpedo-boat flotilla, and so forth. I

[129]

tell you they were a formidable-looking set and evidently dead game fighters!

A PRESIDENT AS COOK

White House, June 11, 1905.

DEAR KERMIT:

Mother and I have just come home from a lovely trip to "Pine Knot." It is really a perfectly delightful little place; the nicest little place of the kind you can imagine. Mother is a great deal more pleased with it than any child with any toy I ever saw. She went down the day before, Thursday, and I followed on Friday morning. Good Mr. Joe Wilmer met me at the station and we rode on horseback to "Round Top," where we met Mother and Mr. Willie Wilmer. We all had tea there and then drove to "Plain Dealing," where we had dinner. Of course I loved both "Round Top" and "Plain Dealing," and as for the two Mr. Wilmers, they are the most generous, thoughtful, self-effacing friends that any one could wish to see. After dinner we went over to "Pine Knot," put everything to

order and went to bed. Next day we spent all
by ourselves at "Pine Knot." In the morning I
fried bacon and eggs, while Mother boiled the
kettle for tea and laid the table. Breakfast was
most successful, and then Mother washed the
dishes and did most of the work, while I did odd
jobs. Then we walked about the place, which is
fifteen acres in all, saw the lovely spring, admired
the pine trees and the oak trees, and then Mother
lay in the hammock while I cut away some trees
to give us a better view from the piazza. The
piazza is the real feature of the house. It is
broad and runs along the whole length and the
roof is high near the wall, for it is a continuation
of the roof of the house. It was lovely to sit
there in the rocking-chairs and hear all the birds
by daytime and at night the whippoorwills and
owls and little forest folk.

Inside the house is just a bare wall with one
big room below, which is nice now, and will be
still nicer when the chimneys are up and there is
a fireplace in each end. A rough flight of stairs
leads above, where there are two rooms, separated

by a passageway. We did everything for ourselves, but all the food we had was sent over to us by the dear Wilmers, together with milk. We cooked it ourselves, so there was no one around the house to bother us at all. As we found that cleaning dishes took up an awful time we only took two meals a day, which was all we wanted. On Saturday evening I fried two chickens for dinner, while Mother boiled the tea, and we had cherries and wild strawberries, as well as biscuits and cornbread. To my pleasure Mother greatly enjoyed the fried chicken and admitted that what you children had said of the way I fried chicken was all true. In the evening we sat out a long time on the piazza, and then read indoors and then went to bed. Sunday morning we did not get up until nine. Then I fried Mother some beefsteak and some eggs in two frying-pans, and she liked them both very much. We went to church at the dear little church where the Wilmers' father and mother had been married, dined soon after two at "Plain Dealing," and then were driven over to the station to go back to Wash-

ington. I rode the big black stallion—Chief—
and enjoyed it thoroughly. Altogether we had a
very nice holiday.

I was lucky to be able to get it, for during the
past fortnight, and indeed for a considerable time
before, I have been carrying on negotiations with
both Russia and Japan, together with side negotiations with Germany, France and England, to
try to get the present war stopped. With infinite
labor and by the exercise of a good deal of tact
and judgment—if I do say it myself—I have
finally gotten the Japanese and Russians to agree
to meet to discuss the terms of peace. Whether
they will be able to come to an agreement or not
I can't say. But it is worth while to have obtained the chance of peace, and the only possible
way to get this chance was to secure such an
agreement of the two powers that they would
meet and discuss the terms direct. Of course
Japan will want to ask more than she ought to
ask, and Russia to give less than she ought to
give. Perhaps both sides will prove impracti-
cable. Perhaps one will. But there is the chance

that they will prove sensible, and make a peace, which will really be for the interest of each as things are now. At any rate the experiment was worth trying. I have kept the secret very successfully, and my dealings with the Japanese in particular have been known to no one, so that the result is in the nature of a surprise.

QUENTIN'S QUAINT SAYINGS

Oyster Bay, N. Y., Aug. 26, 1905.

DEAR KERMIT:

Mr. Phil Stewart and Dr. Lambert spent a night here, Quentin greeting the former with most cordial friendship, and in explanation stating that he always liked to get acquainted with everybody. I take Hall to chop, and he plays tennis with Phil and Oliver, and rides with Phil and Quentin. The Plunger (a submarine) has come to the Bay and I am going out in it this afternoon—or rather down on it. N. B.—I have just been down, for 50 minutes; it was very interesting.

Last night I listened to Mother reading "The

Lances of Linwood" to the two little boys and then hearing them their prayers. Then I went into Archie's room, where they both showed all their china animals; I read them Laura E. Richards' poems, including "How does the President take his tea?" They christened themselves Punkey Doodle and Jollapin, from the chorus of this, and immediately afterwards I played with them on Archie's bed. First I would toss Punkey Doodle (Quentin) on Jollapin (Archie) and tickle Jollapin while Punkey Doodle squalled and wiggled on top of him, and then reverse them and keep Punkey Doodle down by heaving Jollapin on him, while they both kicked and struggled until my shirt front looked very much the worse for wear. You doubtless remember yourself how bad it was for me, when I was dressed for dinner, to play with all you scamps when you were little.

The other day a reporter asked Quentin something about me; to which that affable and canny young gentleman responded, "Yes, I see him sometimes; but I know nothing of his family life."

ADVICE REGARDING NEWSPAPER ANNOYANCES

When Theodore Roosevelt, Jr., entered Harvard as a freshman he had to pay the penalty of being a President's son. Newspaper reporters followed all his movements, especially in athletics, and he was the victim of many exaggerated and often purely fictitious accounts of his doings. His father wrote him indignant and sympathetic letters, two of which are reproduced here.

BLESSED OLD TED: White House, October 2, 1905.

The thing to do is to go on just as you have evidently been doing, attract as little attention as possible, do not make a fuss about the newspaper men, camera creatures, and idiots generally, letting it be seen that you do not like them and avoid them, but not letting them betray you into any excessive irritation. I believe they will soon drop you, and it is just an unpleasant thing that you will have to live down. Ted, I have had an enormous number of unpleasant things that I have had to live down in my life at different times and you have begun to have them now. I saw that you were not out on the football field on Saturday and was rather glad of it, as evidently those infernal idiots were eagerly waiting for you, but whenever you do go you will have to make up your mind that they will make it exceedingly unpleasant for you for once or twice, and you will just have to bear it; for you can never in the world afford to let them drive you away from anything you intend to do, whether it is football or anything else, and by going about your own business quietly and pleasantly, doing just what you would do if they were not there, generally they will get tired of it, and the boys themselves will see that it is not your fault, and will feel, if anything, rather a sympathy for you. Meanwhile I want you to know that we are all thinking of you and sympathizing with you the whole time; and it is a great comfort to me to have such confidence in you and to know that though these creatures can cause you a little trouble and make you feel a little downcast, they can not drive you one way or the other, or make you alter the course you have set out for yourself.

We were all of us, I am almost ashamed to say, rather blue at getting back in the White House, simply because we missed Sagamore Hill so much. But it is very beautiful and we feel very ungrateful at having even a passing fit of blueness, and we are enjoying it to the full now. I have just seen Archie dragging some fifty foot of hose pipe across the tennis court to play in the sand-box. I have been playing tennis with Mr. Pinchot, who beat me three sets to one, the only deuce-set being the one I won.

This is just an occasion to show the stuff there is in you. Do not let these newspaper creatures and kindred idiots drive you one hair's breadth from the line you had marked out in football or anything else. Avoid any fuss, if possible.

DEAR TED: White House, October 11, 1905.

I was delighted to find from your last letters that you are evidently having a pretty good time in spite of the newspaper and kodak creatures. I guess that nuisance is now pretty well abated. Every now and then they will do something horrid; but I think you can safely, from now on, ignore them entirely.

I shall be interested to hear how you get on, first of all with your studies, in which you seem to have started well, and next with football. I expected that you would find it hard to compete with the other candidates for the position of end, as they are mostly heavier than you; especially since you went off in weight owing to the excitement of your last weeks of holdiay in the summer. Of course the fact that you are comparatively light tells against you and gives you a good deal to overcome; and undoubtedly it was from this standpoint not a good thing that you were unable to lead a quieter life toward the end of your stay at Oyster Bay.

So it is about the polo club. In my day we looked with suspicion upon all freshman societies, and the men who tried to get them up or were prominent in them rarely amounted to much in the class afterwards; and it has happened that I have heard rather unfavorably of the polo club. But it may be mere accident that I have thus heard unfavorably about it, and in thirty years the attitude of the best fellows in college to such a thing as a freshman club may have changed so absolutely that my experience can be of no value. Exercise your own best judgment and form some idea of what the really best fellows in the class think on the subject. Do not make the mistake of thinking that the men who are merely undeveloped are really the best fellows, no matter how pleasant and agreeable they are or how popular. Popularity is a good thing, but it is not something for which to sacrifice studies or athletics or good standing in any way; and sometimes to seek it overmuch is to lose it. I do not mean this as applying to you, but as applying to certain men who still have a great vogue at first in the class, and of whom you will naturally tend to think pretty well.

In all these things I can only advise you in a very general way. You are on the ground. You know the men and the general college sentiment. You have gone in with the serious purpose of doing decently and honorably; of standing well in your studies; of showing that in athletics you mean business up to the extent of your capacity, and of getting the respect and liking of your class-mates so far as they can be legitimately obtained. As to the exact methods of carrying out these objects, I must trust to you.

INCIDENTS OF A SOUTHERN TRIP

DEAR KERMIT: White House, Nov. 1, 1905.

I had a great time in the South, and it was very nice indeed having Mr. John McIlhenny and Mr. John Greenway with me. Of course I enjoyed most the three days when Mother was there. But I was so well received and had so many things to say which I was really glad to say, that the whole trip was a success. When I left New Orleans on the little lighthouse tender to go down to the gulf where the big war ship was awaiting me, we had a collision. I was standing up at the time and the shock pitched me forward so that I dove right through the window, taking the glass all out except a jagged rim round the very edge. But I went through so quickly that I received only some minute scratches on my face and hands which, however, bled pretty freely. I was very glad to come up the coast on the squadron of great armored cruisers.

In the gulf the weather was hot and calm, but soon after rounding Florida and heading northward we ran into a gale. Admiral Brownson is a regular little gamecock and he drove the vessels to their limit. It was great fun to see the huge warcraft pounding steadily into the gale and forging onward through the billows. Some of the waves were so high that the water came green over the flying bridge forward, and some of the officers were thrown down and badly bruised. One of the other ships lost a man overboard, and although we hunted for him an hour and a half we could not get him, and had a boat smashed in the endeavor.

When I got back here I found sister, very interesting about her Eastern trip. She has had a great time, and what is more, she has behaved mighty well under rather trying circumstances.

Ethel was a dear, as always, and the two little boys were as cunning as possible. Sister had brought them some very small Japanese fencing armor, which they had of course put on with glee, and were clumsily fencing with wooden two-handed swords. And they had also rigged up in the dark nursery a grewsome man with a pumpkin head, which I was ushered in to see, and in addition to the regular eyes, nose, and saw-tooth mouth, Archie had carved in the back of the pumpkin the words "Pumpkin Giant," the candle inside illuminating it beautifully. Mother was waiting for me at the Navy Yard, looking too pretty for anything, when I arrived. She and I had a ride this afternoon. Of course I am up to my ears in work.

The mornings are lovely now, crisp and fresh; after breakfast Mother and I walk around the grounds accompanied by Skip, and also by Slipper, her bell tinkling loudly. The gardens are pretty dishevelled now, but the flowers that are left are still lovely; even yet some honeysuckle is blooming on the porch.

POETS AND PRINCES

DEAR KERMIT: White House, November 6, 1905.

Just a line, for I really have nothing to say this week. I have caught up with my work. One day we had a rather forlorn little poet and his nice wife in at lunch. They made me feel quite badly by being so grateful at my having mentioned him in what I fear was **a** very patronizing and, indeed, almost supercilious way, as having written an occasional good poem. I am much struck by Robinson's two poems which you sent Mother. What a queer, mystical creature he is! I did not understand one of them—that about the gardens —and I do not know that I like either of them quite as much as some of those in "The Children of the Night." But he certainly has got the real spirit of poetry in him. Whether he can make it come out I am not quite sure.

Prince Louis of Battenberg has been here and I have been very much pleased with him. He is a really good admiral, and in addition he is a well-read and cultivated man and it was charming to talk with him. We had him and his nephew, Prince Alexander, a midshipman, to lunch alone with us, and we really enjoyed having them. At the State dinner he sat between me and Bonaparte, and I could not help smiling to myself in thinking that here was this British Admiral seated beside the American Secretary of the Navy—the American Secretary of the Navy being the grand-nephew of Napoleon and the grandson of Jerome, King of Westphalia; while the British Admiral was the grandson of a Hessian general who was the subject of King Jerome and served under Napoleon, and then, by no means creditably, deserted him in the middle of the Battle of Leipsic.

I am off to vote to-night.

NOVELS AND GAMES

DEAR KERMIT: White House, November 19, 1905.

I sympathize with every word you say in your letter, about Nicholas Nickleby, and about novels generally. Normally I only care for a novel if the ending is good, and I quite agree with you

that if the hero has to die he ought to die worthily
and nobly, so that our sorrow at the tragedy shall
be tempered with the joy and pride one always
feels when a man does his duty well and bravely.
There is quite enough sorrow and shame and suffering and baseness in real life, and there is no
need for meeting it unnecessarily in fiction. As
Police Commissioner it was my duty to deal with
all kinds of squalid misery and hideous and unspeakable infamy, and I should have been worse
than a coward if I had shrunk from doing what
was necessary; but there would have been no use
whatever in my reading novels detailing all this
misery and squalor and crime, or at least in reading them as a steady thing. Now and then there
is a powerful but sad story which really is interesting and which really does good; but normally
the books which do good and the books which
healthy people find interesting are those which
are not in the least of the sugar-candy variety,
but which, while portraying foulness and suffering when they must be portrayed, yet have a
joyous as well as a noble side.

We have had a very mild and open fall. I have played tennis a good deal, the French Ambassador being now quite a steady playmate, as he and I play about alike; and I have ridden with Mother a great deal. Last Monday when Mother had gone to New York I had Selous, the great African hunter, to spend the day and night. He is a perfect old dear; just as simple and natural as can be and very interesting. I took him, with Bob Bacon, Gifford Pinchot, Ambassador Meyer and Jim Garfield, for a good scramble and climb in the afternoon, and they all came to dinner afterwards. Before we came down to dinner I got him to spend three-quarters of an hour in telling delightfully exciting lion and hyena stories to Ethel, Archie and Quentin. He told them most vividly and so enthralled the little boys that the next evening I had to tell them a large number myself.

To-day is Quentin's birthday and he loved his gifts, perhaps most of all the weest, cunningest live pig you ever saw, presented him by Straus. Phil Stewart and his wife and boy, Wolcott (who is Archie's age), spent a couple of nights here. One afternoon we had hide-and-go-seek, bringing down Mr. Garfield and the Garfield boys, and Archie turning up with the entire football team, who took a day off for the special purpose. We had obstacle races, hide-and-go-seek, blind-man's buff, and everything else; and there were times when I felt that there was a perfect shoal of small boys bursting in every direction up and down stairs, and through and over every conceivable object.

Mother and I still walk around the grounds every day after breakfast. The gardens, of course, are very, very dishevelled now, the snap-dragons holding out better than any other flowers.

CHRISTMAS PRESENT TO HIS OLD NURSE
(To Mrs. Dora Watkins)

White House, December 19, 1905.

DEAR DOLLY:

I wish you a merry Christmas, and want you to buy whatever you think you would like with the enclosed check for twenty dollars. It is now just forty years since you stopped being my nurse, when I was a little boy of seven, just one year younger than Quentin now is.

I wish you could see the children play here in the White House grounds. For the last three days there has been snow, and Archie and Quentin and their cousin, cunning little Sheffield Cowles, and their other cousin, Mr. John Elliott's little girl, Helena, who is a perfect little dear, have been having all kinds of romps in the snow—coasting, having snowball fights, and doing everything—in the grounds back of the White House. This coming Saturday afternoon I have agreed to have a great play of hide-and-go-seek in the White House itself, not only with these children but with their various small friends.

DICKENS AND THACKERAY

DEAR KERMIT: White House, February 3, 1906.

I agree pretty well with your views of David Copperfield. Dora was very cunning and attractive, but I am not sure that the husband would

retain enough respect for her to make life quite
what it ought to be with her. This is a harsh
criticism and I have known plenty of women of
the Dora type whom I have felt were a good deal
better than the men they married, and I have
seen them sometimes make very happy homes. I
also feel as you do that if a man had to struggle
on and make his way it would be a great deal
better to have some one like Sophie. Do you
recollect that dinner at which David Copperfield
and Traddles were, where they are described as
seated at the dinner, one "in the glare of the red
velvet lady" and the other "in the gloom of
Hamlet's aunt"? I am so glad you like Thackeray. "Pendennis" and "The Newcomes" and
"Vanity Fair" I can read over and over again.

Ted blew in to-day. I think he has been
studying pretty well this term and now he is
through all his examinations but one. He hopes,
and I do, that you will pay what attention you
can to athletics. Play hockey, for instance, and
try to get into shape for the mile run. I know it
is too short a distance for you, but if you will try

for the hare and hounds running and the mile, too, you may be able to try for the two miles when you go to Harvard.

The weather was very mild early in the week. It has turned cold now; but Mother and I had a good ride yesterday, and Ted and I a good ride this afternoon, Ted on Grey Dawn. We have been having a perfect whirl of dinner engagements; but thank heavens they will stop shortly after Sister's wedding.

A TRIBUTE TO ARCHIE

DEAR KERMIT: White House, March 11, 1906.

I agree pretty much to all your views both about Thackeray and Dickens, although you care for some of Thackeray of which I am not personally fond. Mother loves it all. Mother, by the way, has been reading "The Legend of Montrose" to the little boys and they are absorbed in it. She finds it hard to get anything that will appeal to both Archie and Quentin, as they possess such different natures.

I am quite proud of what Archie did the day before yesterday. Some of the bigger boys were throwing a baseball around outside of Mr. Sidwell's school and it hit one of them square in the eye, breaking all the blood-vessels and making an extremely dangerous hurt. The other boys were all rattled and could do nothing, finally sneaking off when Mr. Sidwell appeared. Archie stood by and himself promptly suggested that the boy should go to Dr. Wilmer. Accordingly he scorched down to Dr. Wilmer's and said there was an emergency case for one of Mr. Sidwell's boys, who was hurt in the eye, and could he bring him. Dr. Wilmer, who did not know Archie was there, sent out word to of course do so. So Archie scorched back on his wheel, got the boy (I do not know why Mr. Sidwell did not take him himself) and led him down to Dr. Wilmer's, who attended to his eye and had to send him at once to a hospital, Archie waiting until he heard the result and then coming home. Dr. Wilmer told me about it and said if Archie had not acted with such promptness the boy (who was four or five years older than Archie, by the way) would have lost his sight.

What a heavenly place a sandbox is for two little boys! Archie and Quentin play industriously in it during most of their spare moments when out in the grounds. I often look out of the office windows when I have a score of Senators and Congressmen with me and see them both hard at work arranging caverns or mountains, with runways for their marbles.

Good-bye, blessed fellow. I shall think of you very often during the coming week, and I am so very glad that Mother is to be with you at your confirmation.

PILLOW FIGHTS WITH THE BOYS

DARLING KERMIT: White House, March 19, 1906.

.   .   .   .

During the four days Mother was away I made a point of seeing the children each evening for three-quarters of an hour or so. Archie and Quentin are really great playmates. One night

I came up-stairs and found Quentin playing the pianola as hard as he could, while Archie would suddenly start from the end of the hall where the pianola was, and, accompanied by both the dogs, race as hard as he could the whole length of the White House clean to the other end of the hall and then tear back again. Another evening as I came up-stairs I found Archie and Quentin having a great play, chuckling with laughter, Archie driving Quentin by his suspenders, which were fixed to the end of a pair of woollen reins. Then they would ambush me and we would have a vigorous pillow-fight, and after five or ten minutes of this we would go into Mother's room, and I would read them the book Mother had been reading them, "The Legend of Montrose." We just got through it the very last evening. Both Skip and Jack have welcomed Mother back with frantic joy, and this morning came in and lay on her bed as soon as she had finished breakfast—for she did not come down to either breakfast or lunch, as she is going to spend the night at Baltimore with the Bonapartes.

I was so interested in your reading "Phineas Finn" that I ordered a copy myself. I have also ordered DeQuincey's works, as I find we have not got them at the White House.

.   .   .   .

SORROWS OF SKIP

DARLING ARCHIE: White House, April 1, 1906.

Poor Skip is a very, very lonely little dog without his family. Each morning he comes up to see me at breakfast time and during most of breakfast (which I take in the hall just outside my room) Skip stands with his little paws on my lap. Then when I get through and sit down in the rocking-chair to read for fifteen or twenty minutes, Skip hops into my lap and stays there, just bathing himself in the companionship of the only one of his family he has left. The rest of the day he spends with the ushers, as I am so frightfully busy that I am nowhere long enough for Skip to have any real satisfaction in my companionship. Poor Jack has never come home. We may never know what became of him.

"AN INTERESTING CIRCUS EXPERIENCE"

White House, April 1, 1906.

DARLING ETHEL:

I haven't heard a word from the two new horses, and I rather believe that if there had been any marked improvement in either of them I should have heard. I gather that one at least and probably both would be all right for me if I were twenty years younger, and would probably be all right for Ted now; but of course as things are at present I do not want a horse with which I have an interesting circus experience whenever we meet an automobile, or one which I cannot get to go in any particular direction without devoting an hour or two to the job. So that it looks as if old Rusty would be good enough for me for some time to come. I am going out on him with Senator Lodge this afternoon, and he will be all right and as fresh as paint, for he has been three days in the stable. But to-day is just a glorious spring day—March having ended as it began, with rain and snow—and I will have a good ride. I miss Mother and you children very much, of course, but I believe you are having a good time, and I am really glad you are to see Havana.

A BIG AND LONELY WHITE HOUSE

White House, April 1, 1906.

DARLING QUENTY-QUEE:

Slipper and the kittens are doing finely. I think the kittens will be big enough for you to pet and have some satisfaction out of when you get home, although they will be pretty young still. I miss you all dreadfully, and the house feels big and lonely and full of echoes with nobody but me in it; and I do not hear any small scamps running up and down the hall just as hard as they can; or hear their voices while I am dressing; or suddenly look out through the windows of the office at the tennis ground and see them racing over it or playing in the sand-box. I love you very much.

A NEW PUPPY AND A NEW HORSE

DEAR KERMIT: White House, April 12, 1906.

.   .   .   .

Last night I played "tickley" in their room

with the two little boys. As we rolled and bounced over all three beds in the course of the play, not to mention frantic chases under them, I think poor Mademoiselle was rather appalled at the result when we had finished. Archie's seven-weeks-old St. Bernard puppy has come and it is the dearest puppy imaginable; a huge, soft thing, which Archie carries around in his arms and which the whole family love.

Yesterday I took a first ride on the new horse, Roswell, Captain Lee going along on Rusty as a kind of a nurse. Roswell is not yet four and he is really a green colt and not quite the horse I want at present, as I haven't time to fuss with him, and am afraid of letting the Sergeant ride him, as he does not get on well with him, and there is nobody else in our stable that can ride at all. He is a beautiful horse, a wonderful jumper, and does not pull at all. He shies pretty badly, especially when he meets an automobile; and when he leaves the stable or strikes a road that he thinks will take him home and is not allowed to go down it, he is apt to rear, which I do not like; but I am inclined to think that he will get

over these traits, and if I can arrange to have Lee
handle him a couple of months more, and if Ted
and I can regularly ride him down at Oyster
Bay, I think that he will turn out all right.

Mother and I walk every morning through the
grounds, which, of course, are lovely. Not only
are the song-sparrows and robins singing, but the
white-throated sparrows, who will, I suppose, soon
leave us for the North, are still in full song, and
this morning they waked us up at daybreak singing just outside the window.

A QUENTIN ANECDOTE

DEAR KERMIT: White House, April 22, 1906.

Ted has been as good and cunning as possible.
He has completely recovered from the effects of
having his eye operated upon, and though the eye
itself is a somewhat gruesome object, Ted is in
the highest spirits. He goes back to Harvard
to-day.

.   .   .   .

As I write, Archie and Quentin are busily engaged in the sand-box and I look out across the

tennis-ground at them. If ever there was a heaven-sent treasure to small boys, that sand-box is the treasure. It was very cunning to see the delight various little children took in it at the egg-rolling on Easter Monday. Thanks to our decision in keeping out grown people and stopping everything at one o'clock, the egg-rolling really was a children's festival, and was pretty and not objectionable this year.

The apple trees are now coming into bloom, including that big arched apple tree, under which Mother and I sit, by the fountain, on the stone bench. It is the apple tree that Mother particularly likes. . . .

Did Quentin write his poems after you had gone? I never can recollect whether you have seen them or not. He is a funny small person if ever there was one. The other day we were discussing a really dreadful accident which had happened; a Georgetown young man having taken out a young girl in a canoe on the river, the canoe upset and the girl was drowned; whereupon the young man, when he got home, took what seemed to us an exceedingly cold-blooded method of a special delivery letter to notify her parents. We were expressing our horror at his sending a special delivery letter, and Quentin solemnly chimed in with "Yes, he wasted ten cents." There was a moment's eloquent silence, and then we strove to explain to Quentin that what we were objecting to was not in the least the young man's spendthrift attitude!

As I walk to and from the office now the terrace is fairly fragrant with the scent of the many-colored hyacinths which Mother has put out in boxes on the low stone walls.

.   .   .   .

A VISIT TO WASHINGTON'S BIRTHPLACE

DEAR KERMIT: White House, April 30, 1906.

On Saturday afternoon Mother and I started off on the *Sylph*, Mother having made up her mind I needed thirty-six hours' rest, and we had a delightful time together, and she was just as cunning as she could be. On Sunday Mother and I spent about four hours ashore, taking our lunch and walking up to the monument which marks where the house stood in which Washington was born. It is a simple shaft. Every vestige of the house is destroyed, but a curious and rather pathetic thing is that, although it must be a hundred years since the place was deserted, there are still multitudes of flowers which must have come from those in the old garden. There are iris and narcissus and a little blue flower, with a neat, prim, clean smell that makes one feel as if it ought to be put with lavender into chests of fresh old linen. The narcissus in particular was growing around everywhere, together with real wild flowers like the painted columbine and star of Bethlehem. It was a lovely spot on a headland overlooking a broad inlet from the Potomac. There was also the old graveyard or grave plot in which were the gravestones of Washington's father and mother and grandmother, all pretty nearly ruined. It was lovely warm weather and Mother and I enjoyed our walk through the funny lonely old country. Mocking-birds, meadow-larks, Carolina wrens, cardinals, and field sparrows were singing cheerfully. We came up the river in time to get home last evening. This morning Mother and I walked around the White House grounds as usual.

I think I get more fond of flowers every year. The grounds are now at that high stage of beauty in which they will stay for the next two months. The buckeyes are in bloom, the pink dogwood, and the fragrant lilacs, which are almost the loveliest of the bushes; and then the flowers, including the lily-of-the-valley.

I am dictating in the office. Archie is out by the sandbox playing with the hose. The playing consists in brandishing it around his head and trying to escape the falling water. He escapes about twice out of three times and must now be a perfect drowned rat. (I have just had him in to look at him and he is even more of a drowned rat than I supposed. He has gone out to complete his shower bath under strict promise that immediately afterwards he will go in and change his clothes.)

Quentin is the funniest mite you ever saw and certainly a very original little fellow. He left at Mademoiselle's plate yesterday a large bunch of flowers with the inscription that they were from the fairies to her to reward her for taking care of "two *good, good* boys." Ethel is a dear.

MORE ABOUT DICKENS

White House, May 20, 1906.

DEAR TED:

Mother read us your note and I was interested in the discussion between you and —— over Dickens. Dickens' characters are really to a great extent personified attributes rather than individuals. In consequence, while there are not nearly as many who are actually like people one meets, as for instance in Thackeray, there are a great many more who possess *characteristics* which we encounter continually, though rarely as strongly developed as in the fictional originals. So Dickens' characters last almost as Bunyan's do. For instance, Jefferson Brick and Elijah Pogram and Hannibal Chollop are all real personifications of certain bad tendencies in American life, and I am continually thinking of or alluding to some newspaper editor or Senator or homicidal rowdy by one of these three names. I never met any one exactly like Uriah Heep, but now and then we see individuals show traits which make it easy to describe them, with reference to those traits, as Uriah Heep. It is just the same with Micawber.

Mrs. Nickleby is not quite a real person, but she typifies, in accentuated form, traits which a great many real persons possess, and I am continually thinking of her when I meet them. There are half a dozen books of Dickens which have, I think, furnished more characters which are the constant companions of the ordinary educated man around us, than is true of any other half-dozen volumes published within the same period.

NO PLACE LIKE SAGAMORE HILL

(To Ethel, at Sagamore Hill)

White House, June 11, 1906.

BLESSED ETHEL:

I am very glad that what changes have been made in the house are good, and I look forward so eagerly to seeing them. After all, fond as I am of the White House and much though I have appreciated these years in it, there isn't any place in the world like home—like Sagamore Hill, where things are our own, with our own associations, and where it is real country.

ATTIC DELIGHTS.

BLESSED ETHEL: White House, June 17, 1906.

Your letter delighted me. I read it over twice, and chuckled over it. By George, how entirely I sympathize with your feelings in the attic! I know just what it is to get up into such a place and find the delightful, winding passages where one lay hidden with thrills of criminal delight, when the grownups were vainly demanding one's appearance at some legitimate and abhorred function; and then the once-beloved and half-forgotten treasures, and the emotions of peace and war, with reference to former companions, which they recall.

I am not in the least surprised about the mental telepathy; there is much in it and in kindred things which are real and which at present we do not understand. The only trouble is that it usually gets mixed up with all kinds of fakes.

I am glad the band had a healthy effect in reviving old Bleistein's youth. I shall never forget the intense interest in life he always used to gain when we encountered an Italian with a barrel organ and a bear—a combination that made Renown seek instant refuge in attempted suicide.

I am really pleased that you are going to teach Sunday school. I think I told you that I taught it for seven years, most of the time in a mission class, my pupils being of a kind which furnished me plenty of vigorous excitement.

PRESIDENTIAL RESCUE OF A KITTEN

DARLING ETHEL:
White House, June 24, 1906.

To-day as I was marching to church, with Sloane some 25 yards behind, I suddenly saw two terriers racing to attack a kitten which was walking down the sidewalk. I bounced forward with my umbrella, and after some active work put to flight the dogs while Sloane captured the kitten, which was a friendly, helpless little thing, evidently too well accustomed to being taken care of to know how to shift for itself. I inquired of all the bystanders and of people on the neighboring porches to know if they knew who owned it; but as they all disclaimed, with many grins, any knowledge of it, I marched ahead with it in my arms for about half a block. Then I saw a very nice colored woman and little colored girl looking out of the window of a small house with on the door a dressmaker's advertisement, and I turned and walked up the steps and asked if they did not want the kitten. They said they did, and the little girl welcomed it lovingly; so I felt I had gotten it a home and continued toward church.

Has the lordly Ted turned up yet? Is his loving sister able, unassisted, to reduce the size of his head, or does she need any assistance from her male parent?

Your affectionate father,

The Tyrant.

chorus of Offspring (led by daughter)
"For he is a tyrant being!"

SPORTS OF QUENTIN AND ARCHIE

DEAR KERMIT: Oyster Bay, Aug. 18, 1906.

. . . .

Quentin is the same cheerful pagan philosopher
as ever. He swims like a little duck; rides well;
stands quite severe injuries without complaint,
and is really becoming a manly little fellow.
Archie is devoted to the *Why* (sailboat). The
other day while Mother and I were coming in,
rowing, we met him sailing out, and it was too
cunning for anything. The *Why* looks exactly
like a little black wooden shoe with a sail in it,
and the crew consisted of Archie, of one of his
beloved playmates, a seaman from the *Sylph*, and
of Skip—very alert and knowing.

SKIP AND ARCHIE

DEAR KERMIT: White House, October 23, 1906.

Archie is very cunning and has handicap races
with Skip. He spreads his legs, bends over, and
holds Skip between them. Then he says, "On

your mark, Skip, ready; go!" and shoves Skip back while he runs as hard as he possibly can to the other end of the hall, Skip scrambling wildly with his paws on the smooth floor until he can get started, when he races after Archie, the object being for Archie to reach the other end before Skip can overtake him.

A TURKEY HUNT AT PINE KNOT

White House, November 4, 1906.

DEAR KERMIT:

Just a line to tell you what a nice time we had at Pine Knot. Mother was as happy as she always is there, and as cunning and pretty as possible. As for me, I hunted faithfully through all three days, leaving the house at three o'clock one day, at four the next, and at five the next, so that I began my hunts in absolute night; but fortunately we had a brilliant moon on each occasion. The first two days were failures. I did not see a turkey, and on each occasion when everybody was perfectly certain that I was going to see a turkey, something went wrong and the turkey did not turn up. The last day I was out thirteen hours, and you may imagine how hungry I was when I got back, not to speak of being tired; though fortunately most of the time I was rambling around on horseback, so I was not done out. But in the afternoon at last luck changed, and then for once everything went right. The hunter who was with me marked a turkey in a point of pines stretching down from a forest into an open valley, with another forest on its farther side. I ran down to the end of the point and hid behind a bush. He walked down through the pines and the turkey came out and started to fly across the valley, offering me a beautiful side shot at about thirty-five yards—just the distance for my ten-bore. I killed it dead, and felt mighty happy as it came tumbling down through the air.

In November, 1906, the President, accompanied by Mrs. Roosevelt, went to the Isthmus of Panama, where he spent three days in inspecting the work of building the Panama Canal, returning by way of Porto Rico. The journey was taken on the naval vessel *Louisiana,* and many of his letters to the children were written while on board that vessel and mailed after reaching Colon.

PETS ON SHIPBOARD

On Board U. S. S. *Louisiana,*
On the Way to Panama.
Sunday, November 11, 1906.

BLESSED QUENTIN:

You would be amused at the pets they have aboard this ship. They have two young bulldogs, a cat, three little raccoons, and a tiny Cuban goat. They seem to be very amicable with one another, although I think the cat has suspicions of all the rest. The coons clamber about everywhere, and the other afternoon while I was sitting reading, I suddenly felt my finger seized in a pair of soft black paws and found the coon sniffing at it, making me feel a little uncomfortable lest it might think the finger something good to eat. The two puppies play endlessly. One of them belongs to Lieutenant Evans. The crew will not be allowed ashore at Panama or else I know they would pick up a whole raft of other pets there.

[172]

The jackies seem especially fond of the little coons. A few minutes ago I saw one of the jackies strolling about with a coon perched upon his shoulder, and now and then he would reach up his hand and give it a small piece of bread to eat.

NAMES OF THE GUNS

On Board U. S. S. *Louisiana,*
Sunday, November 11, 1906.

BLESSED ARCHIE:

I wish you were along with us, for you would thoroughly enjoy everything on this ship. We have had three days of perfect weather, while this great battleship with her two convoys, the great armored cruisers, *Tennessee* and *Washington,* have steamed steadily in column ahead southward through calm seas until now we are in the tropics. They are three as splendid ships of their class as there are afloat, save only the English Dreadnaught. The *Louisiana* now has her gun-sights and everything is all in good shape for her to begin the practice of the duties which will make her crew as fit for man-of-war's work as the crew of any one of our other first-class battleships.

[173]

The men are such splendid-looking fellows, Americans of the best type, young, active, vigorous, with lots of intelligence. I was much amused at the names of the seven-inch guns, which include *Victor*, *Invincible*, *Peacemaker*, together with *Skidoo*, and also one called *Tedd* and one called *The Big Stick*.

REFLECTIONS ON THE WAY

On Board U. S. S. *Louisiana*,
Nov. 13.

DEAR KERMIT:

So far this trip has been a great success, and I think Mother has really enjoyed it. As for me, I of course feel a little bored, as I always do on shipboard, but I have brought on a great variety of books, and am at this moment reading Milton's prose works, "Tacitus," and a German novel called "Jorn Uhl." Mother and I walk briskly up and down the deck together, or else sit aft under the awning, or in the after cabin, with the gun ports open, and read; and I also spend a good deal of time on the forward bridge, and sometimes on the aft bridge, and of course have gone over the ship to inspect it with the Captain. It is a splendid thing to see one of these men-of-war, and it does really make one proud of one's country. Both the officers and the enlisted men are as fine a set as one could wish to see.

It is a beautiful sight, these three great warships standing southward in close column, and almost as beautiful at night when we see not only the lights but the loom through the darkness of the ships astern. We are now in the tropics and I have thought a good deal of the time over eight years ago when I was sailing to Santiago in the fleet of warships and transports. It seems a strange thing to think of my now being President, going to visit the work of the Panama Canal which I have made possible.

Mother, very pretty and dainty in white summer clothes, came up on Sunday morning to see inspection and review, or whatever they call it, of the men. I usually spend half an hour on deck before Mother is dressed. Then we breakfast together alone; have also taken lunch alone, but at dinner have two or three officers to dine with us. Doctor Rixey is along, and is a perfect dear, as always.

EVENTS SINCE COLUMBUS'S DISCOVERY
November 14th.

The fourth day out was in some respects the most interesting. All the forenoon we had Cuba on our right and most of the forenoon and part of the afternoon Hayti on our left; and in each case green, jungly shores and bold mountains—two great, beautiful, venomous tropic islands. These are historic seas and Mother and I have kept thinking of all that has happened in them since Columbus landed at San Salvador (which we also saw), the Spanish explorers, the buccaneers, the English and Dutch sea-dogs and adventurers, the great English and French fleets, the desperate fighting, the triumphs, the pestilences, of all the turbulence, the splendor and the wickedness, and the hot, evil, riotous life of the old planters and slave-owners, Spanish, French, English, and Dutch;—their extermination of the Indians, and bringing in of negro slaves, the decay of most of

[176]

the islands, the turning of Hayti into a land of savage negroes, who have reverted to voodooism and cannibalism; the effort we are now making to bring Cuba and Porto Rico forward.

To-day is calm and beautiful, as all the days have been on our trip. We have just sighted the highest land of Panama ahead of us, and we shall be at anchor by two o'clock this afternoon; just a little less than six days from the time we left Washington.

PRIDE IN AMERICA

On Board U. S. S. *Louisiana*,
Nov. 14.

DEAR TED:

I am very glad to have taken this trip, although as usual I am bored by the sea. Everything has been smooth as possible, and it has been lovely having Mother along. It gives me great pride in America to be aboard this great battleship and to see not only the material perfection of the ship herself in engines, guns and all arrangements, but the fine quality of the officers and crew. Have you ever read Smollett's novel, I think

[177]

"Roderick Random" or "Humphrey Clinker," in which the hero goes to sea? It gives me an awful idea of what a floating hell of filth, disease, tyranny, and cruelty a war-ship was in those days. Now every arrangement is as clean and healthful as possible. The men can bathe and do bathe as often as cleanliness requires. Their fare is excellent and they are as self-respecting a set as can be imagined. I am no great believer in the superiority of times past; and I have no question that the officers and men of our Navy now are in point of fighting capacity better than in the times of Drake and Nelson; and morally and in physical surroundings the advantage is infinitely in our favor.

It was delightful to have you two or three days at Washington. Blessed old fellow, you had a pretty hard time in college this fall; but it can't be helped, Ted; as one grows older the bitter and the sweet keep coming together. The only thing to do is to grin and bear it, to flinch as little as possible under the punishment, and to keep pegging steadily away until the luck turns.

WHAT THE PRESIDENT SAW AT PANAMA

U. S. S. *Louisiana,*
At Sea, November 20, 1906.

DEAR KERMIT:

Our visit to Panama was most successful as well as most interesting. We were there three days and we worked from morning till night. The second day I was up at a quarter to six and got to bed at a quarter of twelve, and I do not believe that in the intervening time, save when I was dressing, there were ten consecutive minutes when I was not busily at work in some shape or form. For two days there [were] uninterrupted tropic rains without a glimpse of the sun, and the Chagres River rose in a flood, higher than any for fifteen years; so that we saw the climate at its worst. It was just what I desired to do.

It certainly adds to one's pleasure to have read history and to appreciate the picturesque. When on Wednesday we approached the coast, and the jungle-covered mountains looked clearer and clearer until we could see the surf beating on the shores, while there was hardly a sign of human

[179]

habitation, I kept thinking of the four centuries of wild and bloody romance, mixed with abject squalor and suffering, which had made up the history of the Isthmus until three years ago. I could see Balboa crossing at Darien, and the wars between the Spaniards and the Indians, and the settlement and the building up of the quaint walled Spanish towns; and the trade, across the seas by galleon, and over land by pack-train and river canoe, in gold and silver, in precious stones; and then the advent of the buccaneers, and of the English seamen, of Drake and Frobisher and Morgan, and many, many others, and the wild destruction they wrought. Then I thought of the rebellion against the Spanish dominion, and the uninterrupted and bloody wars that followed, the last occurring when I became President; wars, the victorious heroes of which have their pictures frescoed on the quaint rooms of the palace at Panama city, and in similar palaces in all capitals of these strange, turbulent little half-caste civilizations. Meanwhile the Panama railroad had been built by Americans over a half century ago, with appalling loss of life, so that it is said, of course with exaggeration, that every sleeper laid represented the death of a man. Then the French canal company started work, and for two or three years did a good deal, until it became evident that the task far exceeded its powers; and then to miscalculation and inefficiency was added the hideous greed of adventurers, trying each to save something from the general wreck, and the company closed with infamy and scandal.

Now we have taken hold of the job. We have difficulties with our own people, of course. I haven't a doubt that it will take a little longer and cost a little more than men now appreciate, but I believe that the work is being done with a very high degree both of efficiency and honesty; and I am immensely struck by the character of American employees who are engaged, not merely in superintending the work, but in doing all the jobs that need skill and intelligence. The steam shovels, the dirt trains, the machine shops, and the like, are all filled with American engineers, conductors, machinists, boiler-makers, carpenters.

From the top to the bottom these men are so
hardy, so efficient, so energetic, that it is a real
pleasure to look at them. Stevens, the head engineer, is a big fellow, a man of daring and good
sense, and burly power. All of these men are
quite as formidable, and would, if it were necessary, do quite as much in battle as the crews of
Drake and Morgan; but as it is, they are doing
a work of infinitely more lasting consequence.
Nothing whatever remains to show what Drake
and Morgan did. They produced no real effect
down here, but Stevens and his men are changing
the face of the continent, are doing the greatest
engineering feat of the ages, and the effect of
their work will be felt while our civilization lasts.
I went over everything that I could possibly go
over in the time at my disposal. I examined
the quarters of married and single men, white
men and negroes. I went over the ground of
the Gatun and La Boca dams; went through
Panama and Colon, and spent a day in the Culebra
cut, where the great work is being done. There
the huge steam-shovels are hard at it; scooping

huge masses of rock and gravel and dirt previously loosened by the drillers and dynamite blasters, loading it on trains which take it away to some dump, either in the jungle or where the dams are to be built. They are eating steadily into the mountain, cutting it down and down. Little tracks are laid on the side-hills, rocks blasted out, and the great ninety-five ton steam-shovels work up like mountain howitzers until they come to where they can with advantage begin their work of eating into and destroying the mountainside. With intense energy men and machines do their task, the white men supervising matters and handling the machines, while the tens of thousands of black men do the rough manual labor where it is not worth while to have machines do it. It is an epic feat, and one of immense significance.

The deluge of rain meant that many of the villages were knee-deep in water, while the flooded rivers tore through the tropic forests. It is a real tropic forest, palms and bananas, bread-fruit trees, bamboos, lofty ceibas, and gorgeous butterflies and brilliant colored birds fluttering among the orchids. There are beautiful flowers, too.

All my old enthusiasm for natural history seemed to revive, and I would have given a good deal to have stayed and tried to collect specimens. It would be a good hunting country too; deer, and now and then jaguars and tapir, and great birds that they call wild turkeys; there are alligators in the rivers. One of the trained nurses from a hospital went to bathe in a pool last August and an alligator grabbed him by the legs and was making off with him, but was fortunately scared away, leaving the man badly injured.

I tramped everywhere through the mud. Mother did not do the roughest work, and had time to see more of the really picturesque and beautiful side of the life, and really enjoyed herself.

P. S. The Gatun dam will make a lake miles long, and the railroad now goes on what will be the bottom of this lake, and it was curious to think that in a few years great ships would be floating in water 100 feet above where we were.

ON THE WAY TO PORTO RICO

U. S. S. *Louisiana*,
At Sea, November 20, 1906.

DEAR TED:

This is the third day out from Panama. We have been steaming steadily in the teeth of the trade wind. It has blown pretty hard, and the ship has pitched a little, but not enough to make either Mother or me uncomfortable.

Panama was a great sight. In the first place it was strange and beautiful with its mass of luxuriant tropic jungle, with the treacherous tropic rivers trailing here and there through it; and it was lovely to see the orchids and brilliant butterflies and the strange birds and snakes and lizards, and finally the strange old Spanish towns and the queer thatch and bamboo huts of the ordinary natives. In the next place it is a tremendous sight to see the work on the canal going on. From the chief engineer and the chief sanitary officer down to the last arrived machinist or time-keeper, the five thousand Americans at work on the Isthmus seemed to me an excep-

tionally able, energetic lot, some of them grumbling, of course, but on the whole a mighty good
lot of men. The West Indian negroes offer a
greater problem, but they are doing pretty well
also. I was astonished at the progress made.
We spent the three days in working from dawn
until long after darkness—dear Dr. Rixey being,
of course, my faithful companion. Mother would
see all she liked and then would go off on a little
spree by herself, and she enjoyed it to the full.

WHAT HE SAW IN PORTO RICO

U. S. S. *Louisiana*,
At Sea, November 23, 1906.

DEAR KERMIT:

We had a most interesting two days at Porto
Rico. We landed on the south side of the island
and were received by the Governor and the rest
of the administration, including nice Mr. Laurance
Grahame; then were given a reception by the
Alcalde and people of Ponce; and then went
straight across the island in automobiles to San
Juan on the north shore. It was an eighty mile
trip and really delightful. The road wound up

to the high mountains of the middle island, through them, and then down again to the flat plain on the north shore. The scenery was beautiful. It was as thoroughly tropical as Panama but much more livable. There were palms, tree-ferns, bananas, mangoes, bamboos, and many other trees and multitudes of brilliant flowers. There was one vine called the dream-vine with flowers as big as great white water-lilies, which close up tight in the day-time and bloom at night. There were vines with masses of brilliant purple and pink flowers, and others with masses of little white flowers, which at night-time smell deliciously. There were trees studded over with huge white flowers, and others, the flamboyants such as I saw in the campaign at Santiago, are a mass of large scarlet blossoms in June, but which now had shed them. I thought the tree-ferns especially beautiful. The towns were just such as you saw in Cuba, quaint, brilliantly colored, with the old church or cathedral fronting the plaza, and the plaza always full of flowers. Of course the towns are dirty, but they are not nearly as dirty and

offensive as those of Italy; and there is something
pathetic and childlike about the people. We are
giving them a good government and the island
is prospering. I never saw a finer set of young
fellows than those engaged in the administration.
Mr. Grahame, whom of course you remember, is
the intimate friend and ally of the leaders of the
administration, that is of Governor Beekman
Winthrop and of the Secretary of State, Mr. Regis
Post. Grahame is a perfect trump and such a
handsome, athletic fellow, and a real Sir Galahad.
Any wrong-doing, and especially any cruelty
makes him flame with fearless indignation. He
perfectly delighted the Porto Ricans and also
immensely puzzled them by coming in his Scotch
kilt to a Government ball. Accordingly, at my
special request, I had him wear his kilt at the
state dinner and reception the night we were at
the palace. You know he is a descendant of Montrose, and although born in Canada, his parents
were Scotch and he was educated in Scotland.
Do tell Mr. Bob Fergie about him and his kilts
when you next write him.

We spent the night at the palace, which is half
palace and half castle, and was the residence of
the old Spanish governors. It is nearly four hundred years old, and is a delightful building, with
quaint' gardens and a quaint sea-wall looking
over the bay. There were colored lanterns light-
ing up the gardens for the reception, and the view
across the bay in the moonlight was lovely. Our
rooms were as attractive as possible too, except
that they were so very airy and open that we
found it difficult to sleep—not that that much
mattered as, thanks to the earliness of our start
and the lateness of our reception, we had barely
four hours in which we even tried to sleep.

The next morning we came back in automobiles
over different and even more beautiful roads.
The mountain passes through and over which
we went made us feel as if we were in a tropic
Switzerland. We had to cross two or three rivers
where big cream-colored oxen with yokes tied
to their horns pulled the automobiles through
the water. At one funny little village we had an
open air lunch, very good, of chicken and eggs

and bread, and some wine contributed by a wealthy
young Spaniard who rode up from a neighboring
coffee ranch.

Yesterday afternoon we embarked again, and
that evening the crew gave a theatrical entertainment on the afterdeck, closing with three
boxing bouts. I send you the program. It was
great fun, the audience being equally enraptured
with the sentimental songs about the flag, and
the sailor's true love and his mother, and with
the jokes (the most relished of which related to
the fact that bed-bugs were supposed to be so
large that they had to be shot!) and the skits
about the commissary and various persons and
deeds on the ship. In a way the freedom of com-
ment reminded me a little of the Roman triumphs,
when the excellent legendaries recited in verse
and prose, anything they chose concerning the
hero in whose deeds they had shared and whose
triumphs they were celebrating. The stage, well
lighted, was built on the aftermost part of the
deck. We sat in front with the officers, and the
sailors behind us in masses on the deck, on the

[190]

aftermost turrets, on the bridge, and even in the fighting top of the aftermost mast. It was interesting to see their faces in the light.

. . . .

P. S. I forgot to tell you about the banners and inscriptions of welcome to me in Porto Rico. One of them which stretched across the road had on it "Welcome to Theodore and Mrs. Roosevelt." Last evening I really enjoyed a rather funny experience. There is an Army and Navy Union composed chiefly of enlisted men, but also of many officers, and they suddenly held a "garrison" meeting in the torpedo-room of this ship. There were about fifty enlisted men together with the Captain and myself. I was introduced as "comrade and shipmate Theodore Roosevelt, President of the United States." They were such a nice set of fellows, and I was really so pleased to be with them; so self-respecting, so earnest, and just the right type out of which to make the typical American fighting man who is also a good citizen. The meeting reminded me a good deal of a lodge meeting at Oyster Bay;

and of course those men are fundamentally of the same type as the shipwrights, railroad men and fishermen whom I met at the lodge, and who, by the way, are my chief backers politically and are the men who make up the real strength of this nation.

SICKNESS OF ARCHIE

White House, March 3, 1907.

DEAR KERMIT:

Poor little Archie has diphtheria, and we have had a wearing forty-eight hours. Of course it is harder upon Mother a good deal than upon me, because she spends her whole time with him together with the trained nurse, while I simply must attend to my work during these closing hours of Congress (I have worked each day steadily up to half past seven and also in the evening); and only see Archiekins for twenty minutes or a half hour before dinner. The poor little fellow likes to have me put my hands on his forehead, for he says they smell so clean and soapy! Last night he was very sick, but this morning he is better, and Dr. Rixey thinks everything is going

[192]

well. Dr. Lambert is coming on this afternoon to see him. Ethel, who is away at Philadelphia, will be sent to stay with the Rixeys. Quentin, who has been exposed somewhat to infection, is not allowed to see other little boys, and is leading a career of splendid isolation among the ushers and policemen.

Since I got back here I have not done a thing except work as the President must during the closing days of a session of Congress. Mother was, fortunately, getting much better, but now of course is having a very hard time of it nursing darling little Archie. He is just as good as gold —so patient and loving. Yesterday that scamp Quentin said to Mademoiselle: "If only I had *Archie's* nature, and *my* head, wouldn't it be great?"

In all his sickness Archie remembered that to-day was Mademoiselle's birthday, and sent her his love and congratulations—which promptly reduced good Mademoiselle to tears.

AT THE JAMESTOWN EXPOSITION

White House, April 29, 1907.

DEAREST KERMIT:

We really had an enjoyable trip to Jamestown. The guests were Mother's friend, Mrs. Johnson, a Virginia lady who reminds me so much of Aunt Annie, my mother's sister, who throughout my childhood was almost as much associated in our home life as my mother herself; Justice Moody, who was as delightful as he always is, and with whom it was a real pleasure to again have a chance to talk; Mr. and Mrs. Bob Bacon, who proved the very nicest guests of all and were companionable and sympathetic at every point. Ethel was as good as gold and took much off of Mother's shoulders in the way of taking care of Quentin. Archie and Quentin had, of course, a heavenly time; went everywhere, below and aloft, and ate indifferently at all hours, both with the officers and enlisted men. We left here Thursday afternoon, and on Friday morning passed in review through the foreign fleet and our own fleet of sixteen great battleships in addition to cruisers. It was an inspiring sight and one I would not

[194]

have missed for a great deal. Then we went in a launch to the Exposition where I had the usual experience in such cases, made the usual speech, held the usual reception, went to the usual lunch, etc., etc.

In the evening Mother and I got on the *Sylph* and went to Norfolk to dine. When the *Sylph* landed we were met by General Grant to convoy us to the house. I was finishing dressing, and Mother went out into the cabin and sat down to receive him. In a minute or two I came out and began to hunt for my hat. Mother sat very erect and pretty, looking at my efforts with a tolerance that gradually changed to impatience. Finally she arose to get her own cloak, and then I found that she had been sitting gracefully but firmly on the hat herself—it was a crush hat and it had been flattened until it looked like a wrinkled pie. Mother did not see what she had done so I speechlessly thrust the hat toward her; but she still did not understand and took it as an inexplicable jest of mine merely saying, "Yes, dear," and with patient dignity, turned and went out of the door with General Grant.

The next morning we went on the *Sylph* up the James River, and on the return trip visited three of the dearest places you can imagine, Shirley, Westover, and Brandon. I do not know whether I loved most the places themselves or the quaint out-of-the-world Virginia gentlewomen in them. The houses, the grounds, the owners, all were too dear for anything and we loved them. That night we went back to the *Mayflower* and returned here yesterday, Sunday, afternoon.

To-day spring weather seems really to have begun, and after lunch Mother and I sat under the apple-tree by the fountain. A purple finch was singing in the apple-tree overhead, and the white petals of the blossoms were silently falling. This afternoon Mother and I are going out riding with Senator Lodge.

GENERAL KUROKI

DEAR KERMIT:... White House, May 12, 1907.

General Kuroki and his suite are here and dined with us at a formal dinner last evening. Everything that he says has to be translated, but nevertheless I had a really interesting talk with him, because I am pretty well acquainted with his campaigns. He impressed me much, as indeed all Japanese military and naval officers do. They are a formidable outfit. I want to try to keep on the best possible terms with Japan and never do her any wrong; but I want still more to see our navy maintained at the highest point of efficiency, for it is the real keeper of the peace.

TEMPORARY ABSENCE OF SKIP

The other day Pete got into a most fearful fight and was dreadfully bitten. He was a very forlorn dog indeed when he came home. And on that particular day Skip disappeared and had not turned up when we went to bed. Poor Archie was very uneasy lest Skip should have gone the way of Jack; and Mother and I shared his uneasiness. But about two in the morning we both of us heard a sharp little bark down-stairs and knew it was Skip, anxious to be let in. So down I went and opened the door on the portico, and

Skip simply scuttled in and up to Archie's room, where Archie waked up enough to receive him literally with open arms and then went to sleep cuddled up to him.

DEATH OF SKIP

Sagamore Hill, Sept. 21, 1907.

BLESSED ARCHIEKINS:

We felt dreadfully homesick as you and Kermit drove away; when we pass along the bay front we always think of the dory; and we mourn dear little Skip, although perhaps it was as well the little doggie should pass painlessly away, after his happy little life; for the little fellow would have pined for you.

Your letter was a great comfort; we'll send on the football suit and hope you'll enjoy the football. Of course it will all be new and rather hard at first.

The house is "put up"; everything wrapped in white that can be, and all the rugs off the floors. Quentin is reduced to the secret service men for steady companionship.

QUENTIN'S SNAKE ADVENTURE

DEAREST ARCHIE: White House, Sept. 28, 1907.

Before we left Oyster Bay Quentin had collected two snakes. He lost one, which did not turn up again until an hour before departure, when he found it in one of the spare rooms. This one he left loose, and brought the other one to Washington, there being a variety of exciting adventures on the way; the snake wriggling out of his box once, and being upset on the floor once. The first day home Quentin was allowed not to go to school but to go about and renew all his friendships. Among other places that he visited was Schmid's animal store, where he left his little snake. Schmid presented him with three snakes, simply to pass the day with—a large and beautiful and very friendly king snake and two little wee snakes. Quentin came hurrying back on his roller skates and burst into the room to show me his treasures. I was discussing certain matters with the Attorney-General at the time, and the snakes were eagerly deposited in my lap. The king snake, by the way, although most friendly with Quentin, had just been making a resolute effort to devour one of the smaller snakes. As Quentin and his menagerie were an interruption to my interview with the Department of Justice, I suggested that he go into the next room, where four Congressmen were drearily waiting until I should be at leisure. I thought that he and his snakes would probably enliven their waiting time. He at once fell in with the suggestion and rushed up to the Congressmen with the assurance that he would there find kindred spirits. They at first thought the snakes were wooden ones, and there was some perceptible recoil when they realized that they were alive. Then the king snake went up Quentin's sleeve—he was three or four feet long—and we hesitated to drag him back because his scales rendered that difficult. The last I saw of Quentin, one Congressman was gingerly helping him off with his jacket, so as to let the snake crawl out of the upper end of the sleeve.

A WESTERN TRIP

In the fall of 1907 the President made a tour through the West and South and went on a hunting-trip in Louisiana. In accordance with his unvarying custom he wrote regularly to his children while on his journeyings.

TRIALS OF A TRAVELLING PRESIDENT

On Board U. S. S. *Mississippi,*
October 1, 1907.

DEAREST ETHEL:

The first part of my trip up to the time that we embarked on the river at Keokuk was just about in the ordinary style. I had continually to rush out to wave at the people at the towns through which the train passed. If the train stopped anywhere I had to make a very short speech to several hundred people who evidently thought they liked me, and whom I really liked, but to whom I had nothing in the world to say. At Canton and Keokuk I went through the usual solemn festivities—the committee of reception and the guard of honor, with the open carriage, the lines of enthusiastic fellow-citizens to whom I bowed continually right and left, the speech

[201]

which in each case I thought went off rather better than I had dared hope—for I felt as if I had spoken myself out. When I got on the boat, however, times grew easier. I still have to rush out continually, stand on the front part of the deck, and wave at groups of people on shore, and at stern-wheel steamboats draped with American flags and loaded with enthusiastic excursionists. But I have a great deal of time to myself, and by gentle firmness I think I have succeeded in impressing on my good hosts that I rather resent allopathic doses of information about shoals and dykes, the amount of sand per cubic foot of water, the quantity of manufactures supplied by each river town, etc.

CHANGES OF THREE CENTURIES

On Board U. S. S. *Mississippi*,
October 1, 1907.

DEAR KERMIT: . . .

After speaking at Keokuk this morning we got aboard this brand new stern-wheel steamer of the regular Mississippi type and started down-stream. I went up on the texas and of course felt an almost irresistible desire to ask the pilot about Mark Twain. It is a broad, shallow, muddy river, at places the channel being barely wide enough for the boat to go through, though to my inexperienced eyes the whole river looks like a channel. The bottom lands, Illinois on one side and Missouri on the other, are sometimes overgrown with forests and sometimes great rich cornfields, with here and there a house, here and there villages, and now and then a little town. At every such place all the people of the neighborhood have gathered to greet me. The water-front of the towns would be filled with a dense packed mass of men, women, and children, waving flags. The little villages have not only their own population, but also the farmers who have driven in in their wagons with their wives and children from a dozen miles back—just such farmers as came to see you and the cavalry on your march through Iowa last summer.

It is my first trip on the Mississippi, and I am greatly interested in it. How wonderful in its rapidity of movement has been the history of our country, compared with the history of the old world. For untold ages this river had been flowing through the lonely continent, not very greatly changed since the close of the Pleistocene. During all these myriads of years the prairie and the forest came down to its banks. The immense herds of the buffalo and the elk wandered along them season after season, and the Indian hunters on foot or in canoes trudged along the banks or skimmed the water. Probably a thousand years saw no change that would have been noticeable to our eyes. Then three centuries ago began the work of change. For a century its effects were not perceptible. Just nothing but an occasional French fleet or wild half savage French-Canadian explorer passing up or down the river or one of its branches in an Indian canoe; then the first faint changes, the building of one or two little French fur traders' hamlets, the passing of one or two British officers' boats, and the very rare appearance of the uncouth American backwoodsman.

Then the change came with a rush. Our settlers reached the head-waters of the Ohio, and flat-boats and keel-boats began to go down to the mouth of the Mississippi, and the Indians and the game they followed began their last great march to the west. For ages they had marched back and forth, but from this march there was never to be a return. Then the day of steamboat traffic began, and the growth of the first American cities and states along the river with their strength and their squalor and their raw pride. Then this mighty steamboat traffic passed its zenith and collapsed, and for a generation the river towns have dwindled compared with the towns which took their importance from the growth of the railroads. I think of it all as I pass down the river.

October 4. . . . We are steaming down the river now between Tennessee and Arkansas. The forest comes down a little denser to the bank, the houses do not look quite so well kept; otherwise there is not much change. There are a dozen steamers accompanying us, filled with delegates from various river cities. The people are all out on the banks to greet us still. Moreover, at night, no matter what the hour is that we pass a town, it is generally illuminated, and sometimes whistles and noisy greetings, while our steamboats whistle in equally noisy response, so that our sleep is apt to be broken. Seventeen governors of different states are along, in a boat by themselves. I have seen a good deal of them, however, and it has been of real use to me, especially as regards two or three problems that are up. At St. Louis there was an enormous multitude of people out to see us. The procession was in a drenching rain, in which I stood bareheaded, smiling affably and waving my drowned hat to those hardy members of the crowd who declined to go to shelter. At Cairo, I was also greeted with great enthusiasm, and I was interested to find that there was still extreme bitterness felt over Dickens's description of the town and the people in "Martin Chuzzlewit" sixty-five years ago.

.   .   .   .

PECULIARITIES OF MISSISSIPPI STEAMBOATS

On Board U. S. S. *Mississippi*,
Oct. 1, 1907.

DEAR ARCHIE: . . .

I am now on what I believe will be my last trip of any consequence while I am President.

[206]

Until I got to Keokuk, Iowa, it was about like any other trip, but it is now pleasant going down the Mississippi, though I admit that I would rather be at home. We are on a funny, stern-wheel steamer. Mr. John McIlhenny is with me, and Capt. Seth Bullock among others. We have seen wild geese and ducks and cormorants on the river, and the people everywhere come out in boats and throng or cluster on the banks to greet us.

October 4. You would be greatly amused at these steamboats, and I think you will like your trip up the Mississippi next spring, if only everything goes right, and Mother is able to make it. There is no hold to the boat, just a flat bottom with a deck, and on this deck a foot or so above the water stands the engine-room, completely open at the sides and all the machinery visible as you come up to the boat. Both ends are blunt, and the gangways are drawn up to big cranes. Of course the boats could not stand any kind of a sea, but here they are very useful, for they are shallow and do not get hurt when they bump into the bank or one another. The river runs down in a broad, swirling, brown current, and nobody but an expert could tell the channel. One pilot or another is up in the *Texas* all day long and all night. Now the channel goes close under one bank, then we have to cross the river and go under the other bank; then there will come a deep spot when we can go anywhere. Then we wind in and out among shoals and sand-bars. At night the steamers are all lighted up, for there are a dozen of them in company with us. It is nice to look back at them as they twist after us in a long winding line down the river.

THE LONE CAT OF THE CAMP

Stamboul, La., Oct. 13, 1907.

DARLING QUENTIN:

When we shifted camp we came down here and found a funny little wooden shanty, put up by some people who now and then come out here and sleep in it when they fish or shoot. The only living thing around it was a pussy-cat. She was most friendly and pleasant, and we found that she had been living here for two years. When people were in the neighborhood, she would take what scraps she could get, but the rest of the time she would catch her own game for herself. She was pretty thin when we came, and has already fattened visibly. She was not in the least disconcerted by the appearance of the hounds, and none of them paid the slightest attention to her when she wandered about among them. We are camped on the edge of a lake. This morning before breakfast I had a good swim in it, the water being warmer than the air, and this evening I rowed on it in the moonlight. Every night we hear the great owls hoot and laugh in uncanny fashion.

Camp on Tenesas Bayou,
Oct. 6, 1907.

DARLING ETHEL:

Here we are in camp. It is very picturesque, and as comfortable as possible. We have a big fly tent for the horses; the hounds sleep with them, or with the donkeys! There is a white hunter, Ben Lily, who has just joined us, who is a really remarkable character. He literally lives in the woods. He joined us early this morning, with one dog. He had tramped for twenty-four hours through the woods, without food or water, and had slept a couple of hours in a crooked tree, like a wild turkey.

He has a mild, gentle face, blue eyes, and full beard; he is a religious fanatic, and is as hardy

as a bear or elk, literally caring nothing for fatigue and exposure, which we couldn't stand at all. He doesn't seem to consider the 24 hours' trip he has just made, any more than I should a half hour's walk before breakfast. He quotes the preacher Talmage continually.

This is a black belt. The people are almost all negroes, curious creatures, some of them with Indian blood, like those in "Voodoo Tales." Yesterday we met two little negresses riding one mule, bare-legged, with a rope bridle.

Tenesas Bayou, Oct. 10, 1907.

BLESSED ARCHIE:

I just loved your letter. I was so glad to hear from you. I was afraid you would have trouble with your Latin. What a funny little fellow Opdyke must be; I am glad you like him. How do you get on at football?

We have found no bear. I shot a deer; I sent a picture of it to Kermit.

A small boy here caught several wildcats. When one was in the trap he would push a box towards it, and it would itself get into it, to hide; and so he would capture it alive. But one, instead of getting into the box, combed the hair of the small boy!

We have a great many hounds in camp; at night they gaze solemnly into the fire.

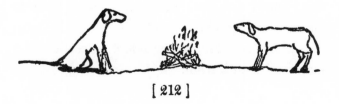

Dr. Lambert has caught a good many bass, which we have enjoyed at the camp table.

DARLING ARCHIE: Bear Bayou, Oct. 16, 1907.

We have had no luck with the bear; but we have killed as many deer as we needed for meat, and the hounds caught a wildcat. Our camp is as comfortable as possible, and we have great camp fires at night.

One of the bear-hunting planters with me told

[213]

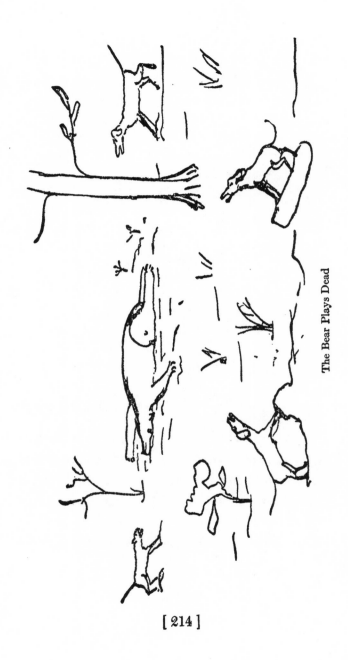

The Bear Plays Dead

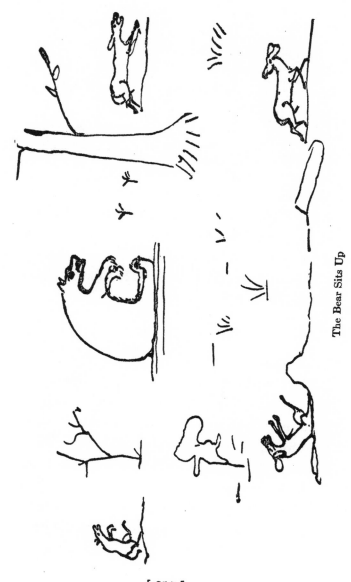

The Bear Sits Up

me he once saw a bear, when overtaken by the hounds, lie down flat on its back with all its legs stretched out, while the dogs barked furiously all around it.

Suddenly the bear sat up with a jump, and frightened all the dogs so that they nearly turned back somersaults.

At this camp there is a nice tame pussy-cat which lies out here all the time, catching birds, mice, or lizards; but very friendly with any party of hunters which happens along.

P. S.—I have just killed a bear; I have written Kermit about it.

SHOOTING THE BEAR

En route to Washington, Oct. 22, 1907.

DEAR TED:

"Bad old father" is coming back after a successful trip. It was a success in every way, including the bear hunt; but in the case of the bear hunt we only just made it successful and no more, for it was not until the twelfth day of steady hunting that I got my bear. Then I shot it in the most approved hunter's style, going up on it in a cane-brake as it made a walking bay before the dogs.

[216]

I also killed a deer—more by luck than anything else, as it was a difficult shot.

QUENTIN'S "EXQUISITE JEST"

White House, Jan. 2, 1908.

DEAR ARCHIE:

Friday night Quentin had three friends, including the little Taft boy, to spend the night with him. They passed an evening and night of delirious rapture, it being a continuous rough-house save when they would fall asleep for an hour or two from sheer exhaustion. I interfered but once, and that was to stop an exquisite jest of Quentin's, which consisted in procuring sulphureted hydrogen to be used on the other boys when they got into bed. They played hard, and it made me realize how old I had grown and how very busy I had been these last few years, to find that they had grown so that I was not needed in the play. Do you recollect how we all of us used to play hide-and-go-seek in the White House? and have obstacle races down the hall when you brought in your friends?

Mother continues much attached to Scamp,

who is certainly a cunning little dog. He is very affectionate, but so exceedingly busy when we are out on the grounds, that we only catch glimpses of him zigzagging at full speed from one end of the place to the other. The kitchen cat and he have strained relations but have not yet come to open hostility.

White House, Jan. 27, 1908.

DEAR ARCHIE:

Scamp is really a cunning little dog, but he takes such an extremely keen interest in hunting, and is so active, that when he is out on the grounds with us we merely catch glimpses of him as he flashes by. The other night after the Judicial Reception when we went up-stairs to supper the kitchen cat suddenly appeared parading down the hall with great friendliness, and was forthwith exiled to her proper home again.

TOM PINCH

White House, February 23, 1908.

DEAREST KERMIT:

I quite agree with you about Tom Pinch. He is a despicable kind of character; just the kind of character Dickens liked, because he had himself a thick streak of maudlin sentimentality of the kind that, as somebody phrased it, "made him wallow naked in the pathetic." It always interests me about Dickens to think how much first-class work he did and how almost all of it was mixed up with every kind of cheap, second-rate matter. I am very fond of him. There are innumerable characters that he has created which symbolize vices, virtues, follies, and the like almost as well as the characters in Bunyan; and therefore I think the wise thing to do is simply to skip the bosh and twaddle and vulgarity and untruth, and get the benefit out of the rest. Of course one fundamental difference between Thackeray and Dickens is that Thackeray was a gentleman and Dickens was not. But a man might do some mighty good work and not be a gentleman in any sense.

"MARTIN CHUZZLEWIT"

DEAREST KERMIT: White House, February 29, 1908.

Of course I entirely agree with you about "Martin Chuzzlewit." But the point seems to me that the preposterous perversion of truth and the ill-nature and malice of the book are of consequence chiefly as indicating Dickens' own character, about which I care not a rap; whereas, the characters in American shortcomings and vices and follies as typified are immortal, and, moreover, can be studied with great profit by all of us to-day. Dickens was an ill-natured, selfish cad and boor, who had no understanding of what the word gentleman meant, and no appreciation of hospitality or good treatment. He was utterly incapable of seeing the high purpose and the real greatness which (in spite of the presence also of much that was bad or vile) could have been visible all around him here in America to any man whose vision was both keen and lofty. He could not see the qualities of the young men growing up here, though it was these qualities that enabled these men to conquer the West and to fight to a finish the great Civil War, and though they were to produce leadership like that of Lincoln, Lee, and Grant. Naturally he would think there was no gentleman in New York, because by no possibility could he have recognized a gentle-

man if he had met one. Naturally he would con-
demn all America because he had not the soul
to see what America was really doing. But he
was in his element in describing with bitter truth-
fulness Scadder and Jefferson Brick, and Elijah
Pogram, and Hannibal Chollup, and Mrs. Hominy
and the various other characters, great and small,
that have always made me enjoy "Martin Chuzzlewit." Most of these characters we still have
with us.

GOOD READING FOR PACIFISTS

DEAREST KERMIT: March 4, 1908.

You have recently been writing me about
Dickens. Senator Lodge gave me the following
first-class quotation from a piece by Dickens about
"Proposals for Amusing Posterity":

"And I would suggest that if a body of gentle-
men possessing their full phrenological share of
the combative and antagonistic organs, could
only be induced to form themselves into a society
for Declaiming about Peace, with a very considerable war-whoop against all non-declaimers;

[221]

and if they could only be prevailed upon to sum up eloquently the many unspeakable miseries and horrors of War, and to present them to their own country as a conclusive reason for its being undefended against War, and becoming a prey of the first despot who might choose to inflict those miseries and horrors—why then I really believe we should have got to the very best joke we could hope to have in our whole Complete Jest-Book for Posterity and might fold our arms and rest convinced that we had done enough for that discerning Patriarch's amusement."

This ought to be read before all the tomfool peace societies and anti-imperialist societies of the present-day.

QUENTIN AS A BALL-PLAYER

DEAREST ARCHIE: White House, March 8, 1908.

Yesterday morning Quentin brought down all his Force School baseball nine to practise on the White House grounds. It was great fun to see them, and Quentin made a run. It reminded me of when you used to come down with the Friend's

[222]

School eleven. Moreover, I was reminded of the occasional rows in the eleven by an outburst in connection with the nine which resulted in their putting off of it a small boy who Quentin assured me was the "meanest kid in town." I like to see Quentin practising baseball. It gives me hopes that one of my boys will not take after his father in this respect, and will prove able to play the national game!

Ethel has a delightful new dog—a white bull terrier—not much more than a puppy as yet. She has named it Mike and it seems very affectionate. Scamp is really an extraordinary ratter, and kills a great many rats in the White House, in the cellars and on the lower floor and among the machinery. He is really a very nice little dog.

DEAREST ARCHIE: White House, March 15, 1908.

Quentin is now taking a great interest in baseball. Yesterday the Force School nine, on which he plays second base, played the P Street nine on the White House grounds where Quentin has marked out a diamond. The Force School nine was victorious by a score of 22 to 5. I told Quentin I was afraid the P Street boys must have felt badly and he answered, "Oh, I guess not; you see I filled them up with lemonade afterward!" Charlie Taft is on his nine.

Did you hear of the dreadful time Ethel had with her new bull terrier, Mike? She was out riding with Fitz Lee, who was on Roswell, and Mike was following. They suppose that Fidelity must have accidentally kicked Mike. The first they knew the bulldog sprang at the little mare's throat. She fought pluckily, rearing and plunging, and shook him off, and then Ethel galloped away. As soon as she halted, Mike overtook her and attacked Fidelity again. He seized her by the shoulder and tried to seize her by the throat, and twice Ethel had to break away and gallop off, Fitz Lee endeavoring in vain to catch the dog. Finally he succeeded, just as Mike had got Fidelity by the hock. He had to give Mike a tremendous beating to restore him to obedience; but of course Mike will have to be disposed of.

Fidelity was bitten in several places and it was a wonder that Ethel was able to keep her seat, because naturally the frightened little mare reared and plunged and ran.

FOUR SHEEPISH SMALL BOYS

DEAREST ARCHIE: White House, April 11, 1908.

Ethel has bought on trial an eight-months bull-dog pup. He is very cunning, very friendly, and wriggles all over in a frantic desire to be petted.

Quentin really seems to be getting on pretty well with his baseball. In each of the last two games he made a base hit and a run. I have just had to give him and three of his associates a dressing down—one of the three being Charlie Taft. Yesterday afternoon was rainy, and four of them played five hours inside the White House. They were very boisterous and were all the time on the verge of mischief, and finally they made spit-balls and deliberately put them on the portraits. I did not discover it until after dinner, and then pulled Quentin out of bed and had him take them all off the portraits, and this morning required him to bring in the three other culprits before me. I explained to them that they had acted like boors; that it would have been a disgrace to have behaved so in any gentleman's house; that Quentin could have no friend to see him, and the other three could not come inside the White House, until I felt that a sufficient time had elapsed to serve as punishment. They were four very sheepish small boys when I got through with them.

JOHN BURROUGHS AND THE FLYING SQUIRRELS

White House, May 10, 1908.

DEAREST ARCHIE:

Mother and I had great fun at Pine Knot. Mr. Burroughs, whom I call Oom John, was with us and we greatly enjoyed having him. But one night he fell into great disgrace! The flying squirrels that were there last Christmas had raised a brood, having built a large nest inside of the room in which you used to sleep and in which John Burroughs slept. Of course they held high carnival at night-time. Mother and I do not

[226]

mind them at all, and indeed rather like to hear them scrambling about, and then as a sequel to a sudden frantic fight between two of them, hearing or seeing one little fellow come plump down to the floor and scuttle off again to the wall. But one night they waked up John Burroughs and he spent a misguided hour hunting for the nest, and when he found it took it down and caught two of the young squirrels and put them in a basket. The next day under Mother's direction I took them out, getting my fingers somewhat bitten in the process, and loosed them in our room, where we had previously put back the nest. I do not think John Burroughs profited by his misconduct, because the squirrels were more active than ever that night both in his room and ours, the disturbance in their family affairs having evidently made them restless!

BEAUTY OF WHITE HOUSE GROUNDS

White House, May 17, 1908.

DEAREST ARCHIE:

Quentin is really doing pretty well with his baseball, and he is perfectly absorbed in it. He

[227]

now occasionally makes a base hit if the opposing pitcher is very bad; and his nine wins more than one-half of its games.

The grounds are too lovely for anything, and spring is here, or rather early summer, in full force. Mother's flower-gardens are now as beautiful as possible, and the iron railings of the fences south of them are covered with clematis and roses in bloom. The trees are in full foliage and the grass brilliant green, and my friends, the warblers, are trooping to the north in full force.

QUENTIN AND A BEEHIVE

White House, May 30, 1908.

DEAREST ARCHIE:

Quentin has met with many adventures this week; in spite of the fact that he has had a bad cough which has tended to interrupt the variety of his career. He has become greatly interested in bees, and the other day started down to get a beehive from somewhere, being accompanied by a mongrel looking small boy as to whose name I inquired. When repeated by Quentin it was

[228]

obviously an Italian name. I asked who he was and Quentin responded: "Oh, his father keeps a fruit-stand." However, they got their bees all right and Quentin took the hive up to a school exhibit. There some of the bees got out and were left behind ("Poor homeless miserables," as Quentin remarked of them), and yesterday they at intervals added great zest to life in the classroom. The hive now reposes in the garden and Scamp surveys it for hours at a time with absorbed interest. After a while he will get to investigating it, and then he will find out more than he expects to.

This afternoon Quentin was not allowed to play ball because of his cough, so he was keeping the score when a foul tip caught him in the eye. It was quite a bad blow, but Quentin was very plucky about it and declined to go in until the game was finished, an hour or so later. By that time his eye had completely shut up and he now has a most magnificent bandage around his head over that eye, and feels much like a baseball hero. I came in after dinner to take a look at him and to my immense amusement found that he was lying flat on his back in bed saying his prayers, while Mademoiselle was kneeling down. It took me a moment or two to grasp the fact that good Mademoiselle wished to impress on him that it was not right to say his prayers unless he knelt down, and as that in this case he could not kneel down she would do it in his place!

QUENTIN AND TURNER
(To Mrs. Nicholas Longworth, Cincinnati, Ohio)
Oyster Bay, June 29, 1908.

. . . .

Quentin is really too funny for anything. He got his legs fearfully sunburned the other day, and they blistered, became inflamed, and ever-faithful Mother had to hold a clinic on him. Eyeing his blistered and scarlet legs, he remarked, "They look like a Turner sunset, don't they?" And then, after a pause, "I won't be caught again this way! quoth the raven, 'Nevermore!'" I was not surprised at his quoting Poe, but I would like to know where the ten-year-old scamp picked up any knowledge of Turner's sunsets.

[230]

QUENTIN AND THE PIG

DEAREST KERMIT: White House, October 17, 1908.

.   .   .   .

Quentin performed a characteristic feat yesterday. He heard that Schmidt, the animal man, wanted a small pig, and decided that he would turn an honest penny by supplying the want. So out in the neighborhood of his school he called on an elderly darkey who, he had seen, possessed little pigs; bought one; popped it into a bag; astutely dodged the school—having a well-founded distrust of how the boys would feel toward his passage with the pig—and took the car for home. By that time the pig had freed itself from the bag, and, as he explained, he journeyed in with a "small squealish pig" under his arm; but as the conductor was a friend of his he was not put off. He bought it for a dollar and sold it to Schmidt for a dollar and a quarter, and feels as if he had found a permanent line of business. Schmidt then festooned it in red ribbons and sent it to parade the streets. I gather that Quentin led

[231]

it around for part of the parade, but he was somewhat vague on this point, evidently being a little
uncertain as to our approval of the move.

A PRESIDENTIAL FALL

White House, Nov. 8, 1908.
DEAREST ARCHIE:

Quentin is getting along very well; he plays
centre on his football eleven, and in a match for
juniors in tennis he got into the semi-finals. What
is more important, he seems to be doing very well
with his studies, and to get on well with the boys,
and is evidently beginning to like the school. He
has shown himself very manly. Kermit is home
now, and is a perfect dear.

The other day while taking a scramble walk
over Rock Creek, when I came to that smooth-
face of rock which we get round by holding on to
the little bit of knob that we call the Button, the
top of this button came off between my thumb
and forefinger. I hadn't supposed that I was
putting much weight on it, but evidently I was,
for I promptly lost my balance, and finding I

was falling, I sprang out into the creek. There were big rocks in it, and the water was rather shallow, but I landed all right and didn't hurt myself the least bit in the world.

MORE ABOUT QUENTIN

DEAREST ARCHIE: White House, Nov. 22, 1908.

I handed your note and the two dollar bill to Quentin, and he was perfectly delighted. It came in very handy, because poor Quentin has been in bed with his leg in a plaster cast, and the two dollars I think went to make up a fund with which he purchased a fascinating little steam-engine, which has been a great source of amusement to him. He is out to-day visiting some friends, although his leg is still in a cast. He has a great turn for mechanics.

BLESSED ARCHIE: White House, Nov. 27, 1908.

It is fine to hear from you and to know you are having a good time. Quentin, I am happy to say, is now thoroughly devoted to his school.

[233]

He feels that he is a real Episcopal High School boy, and takes the keenest interest in everything. Yesterday, Thanksgiving Day, he had various friends here. His leg was out of plaster and there was nothing he did not do. He roller-skated; he practised football; he had engineering work and electrical work; he went all around the city; he romped all over the White House; he went to the slaughter-house and got a pig for Thanksgiving dinner.

Ethel is perfectly devoted to Ace, who adores her. The other day he was lost for a little while; he had gone off on a side street and unfortunately saw a cat in a stable and rushed in and killed it, and they had him tied up there when one of our men found him.

In a way I know that Mother misses Scamp, but in another way she does not, for now all the squirrels are very tame and cunning and are hopping about the lawn and down on the paths all the time, so that we see them whenever we walk, and they are not in the least afraid of us.

DEAREST ARCHIE:

I have a very strong presentiment that Santa Claus will not forget that watch! Quentin went out shooting with Dr. Rixey on Monday and killed three rabbits, which I think was pretty good. He came back very dirty and very triumphant, and Mother, feeling just as triumphant, brought him promptly over with his gun and his three rabbits to see me in the office. On most days now he rides out to school, usually on Achilles. Very shortly he will begin to spend his nights at the school, however. He has become sincerely attached to the school, and at the moment thinks he would rather stay there than go to Groton; but this is a thought he will get over—with Mother's active assistance. He has all kinds of friends, including some who are on a hockey team with him here in the city. The hockey team apparently plays hockey now and then, but only very occasionally, and spends most of the time disciplining its own members.

In 1909, after retiring from the Presidency, Colonel Roosevelt went on a hunting trip in Africa, writing as usual to his children while away.

TRIBUTE TO KERMIT

On the 'Nzor River, Nov. 13, 1909.

DARLING ETHEL:

Here we are, by a real tropical river, with game all around, and no human being within several days' journey. At night the hyenas come round the camp, uttering their queer howls; and once or twice we have heard lions; but unfortunately have never seen them. Kermit killed a leopard yesterday. He has really done so very well! It is rare for a boy with his refined tastes and his genuine appreciation of literature—and of so much else—to be also an exceptionally bold and hardy sportsman. He is still altogether too reckless; but by my hen-with-one-chicken attitude, I think I shall get him out of Africa uninjured; and his keenness, cool nerve, horsemanship, hardihood, endurance, and good eyesight make him a really good wilderness hunter. We have become genuinely attached to Cunninghame and Tarleton, and all three naturalists, especially Heller; and also to our funny black attendants. The porters always amuse us; at this moment about thirty of them are bringing in the wood for the camp fires, which burn all night; and they are all chanting in chorus, the chant being nothing but the words "*Wood*—plenty of wood to burn!"

A Merry Christmas to you! And to Archie and Quentin. How I wish I were to be with you all, no matter how cold it might be at Sagamore; but I suppose we shall be sweltering under mosquito nets in Uganda.

LONGING FOR HOME

Campalla, Dec. 23, 1909.

BLESSEDEST ETHELY-BYE:

Here we are, the most wise Bavian—particularly nice—and the Elderly Parent, on the last stage of their journey. I am enjoying it all, but I think Kermit regards me as a little soft, because I am so eagerly looking forward to the end, when I shall see darling, pretty Mother, my own sweetheart, and the very nicest of all nice daughters—

[237]

you blessed girlie. Do you remember when you explained, with some asperity, that of course you wished Ted were at home, because you didn't have anybody as a really intimate companion, whereas Mother had "old Father"? It is a *great* comfort to have a daughter to whom I can write about all kinds of intimate things!

This is a most interesting place. We crossed the great Nyanza Lake, in a comfortable steamer, in 24 hours, seeing a lovely sunset across the vast expanse of waters; and the moonlight later was as lovely. Here it is as hot as one would expect directly on the Equator, and the brilliant green landscape is fairly painted with even more brilliant flowers, on trees, bush, and vines; while the strange, semi-civilized people are most interesting. The queer little king's Prime Minister, an exceedingly competent, gorgeously dressed, black man, reminds Kermit of a rather civilized Umslopagaar—if that is the way you spell Rider Haggard's Zulu hero.

In this little native town we are driven round in rickshaws, each with four men pushing and pulling, who utter a queer, clanging note of exclamation in chorus, every few seconds, hour after hour.

THE LAST HUNT

DEAREST ARCHIE: Gondokoro, Feb. 27, 1910.

Here, much to my pleasure, I find your letter written after the snow-storm at Sagamore. No snow here! On two or three days the thermometer at noon has stood at 115 degrees in the shade. All three naturalists and Mr. Cunninghame, the guide, have been sick, and so Kermit and I made our last hunt alone, going for eight days into the Lado. We were very successful, getting among other things three giant eland, which are great prizes. We worked hard; Kermit of course worked hardest, for he is really a first-class walker and runner; I had to go slowly, but I kept at it all day and every day. Kermit has really become not only an excellent hunter but also a responsible and trustworthy man, fit to lead; he managed the whole caravan and after hunting all day he would sit up half the night taking care of the skins. He is also the nicest possible companion. We are both very much attached to our gun-bearers and tent boys, and will be sorry to part with them.

QUENTIN GROWN-UP

New York, Dec. 23, 1911.

DEAR ARCHIE:

Quentin turned up last night. He is half an inch taller than I am, and is in great shape. He is much less fat than he was, and seems to be turning out right in every way. I was amused to have him sit down and play the piano pretty well. We miss you dreadfully now that Christmas has come. The family went into revolt about my slouch hat, which Quentin christened "Old Mizzoura," and so I have had to buy another with a less pronounced crown and brim. We all drank your good health at dinner.